LAST GIFT OF THE MAGI

A Christmas Parable for All Seasons

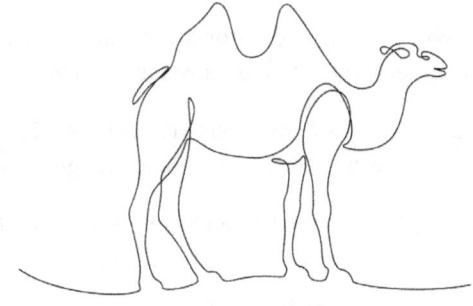

LOUIS A. TARTAGLIA, M.D.

Copyright © 2022 by Louis A. Tartaglia, M.D.

LAST GIFT OF THE MAGI
A CHRISTMAS PARABLE FOR ALL SEASONS

All rights reserved. No part of this publication may be reproduced, distributed, or transmitted in any form or by any means, including photocopying, recording, or other electronic or mechanical methods, without the prior written permission of the publisher, except in the case of brief quotations embodied in critical reviews and certain other noncommercial uses permitted by copyright law.

For permission requests, write to the publisher, addressed "Attention: Permissions Coordinator," carol@markvictorhansenlibrary.com

Quantity sales special discounts are available on quantity purchases by corporations, associations, and others. For details, contact the publisher at carol@markvictorhansenlibrary.com

Orders by U.S. trade bookstores and wholesalers. Email: carol@markvictorhansenlibrary.com

Cover Design - Low & Joe Creative, Brea, CA 92821
Book Layout - DBree, StoneBear Design

Manufactured and printed in the United States of America distributed globally by markvictorhansenlibrary.com

New York | Los Angeles | London | Sydney

ISBN: 979-8-88581-062-3 Hardback
ISBN: 979-8-88581-063-0 Paperback
ISBN: 979-8-88581-064-7 eBook
Library of Congress Cataloging-in-Publication Data has been applied for.

Dedication

To my wife Jeanne Civello-Tartaglia, the Italian American firebrand, gift from God, a delightful being who exemplifies carrying Christ around in all that she does. *Thank you for your encouragement and support.*

Without her love and backing, I would not have had the stability or peace of mind to do what I do.

Acknowledgments

A big thank you to Mark Victor Hanson, who encouraged me to finish this story and has been a friend who has always seen potential in me. He is the most creative being I have ever met. I enjoy our endless hours of banter about any topic that we choose. I always come away feeling better about life.

To Les Brown. We have always considered each other family from that first meeting so many years ago. Our backgrounds were so diverse, but our values, virtues, and flaws were so similar that it was like we grew up in the same family. He has always left me with hope in every interaction we have had.

Notes of Historical Interest

The following information was found at the Universita' Catolica in Rome, Italy, with the help of Father Angelo Scolozzi, Cofounder with Mother Teresa of the Missionaries of Charity, Third Order, now known as the Universal Fraternity of the Word. We had a simple discussion of a tale told by Thomas Merton about the number of Magi. We went searching in the library for some facts. First of all, there were probably twelve Magi, though the Latin names reflect only eight. It turns out that it was not until the Fourth to Sixth century after the birth of Christ that the names Gaspar, Balthasar, and Melchior came into common usage. Some historians believe that the wife of Constantine the Great decided there should be three Magi symbolically representing the Trinity.

THE EASTERN NAMES OF THE MAGI:

India:	Gaspar	Badadilma (Horsed)
	Hormisdas (Arshek)	Cosnasap
Persia:	Balthasar	Akreho
	Arbakchest	Astonkakodon
Arabia:	Melchior	Merodak
	Aksherosh	Sadlak

THE LATIN NAMES OF THE MAGI:

Appellius	Amerius
Damascus	Magalth
Pangalath	Saracen
Ator	Periatorus

Foreword

When I was asked to write a foreword to *The Last Gift of the Magi*, I was concerned that I was not a writer, as was my late husband Og Mandino. I agreed to do it because Dr. Lou Tartaglia was a friend of Og's, and is a good friend of mine. I can remember back to when Lou was writing the Camel as he referred to it. Og had agreed to be his mentor. He was encouraging Lou to get his ideas about life and spiritual development down on paper. Og had fun watching "the Doc" struggle to develop his writing craft. One time he called Lou and told him that he had thrown out the manuscript. "You've got to start over Babe," he said to the stunned psychiatrist.

In some ways, these two men were very similar and yet, in others, they were very different. They both cherish family and friends. They both have a sentimental streak as wide as a highway. They both loved hot pepper with their pasta. Og liked to organize his speeches and stick to his outline. Lou loves to organize his speeches too, but then loves to be extemporaneous. Og was well known, in fact famous. Lou is the best-kept secret in inspirational circles.

As a husband, father, friend, and author, Og will be deeply missed. He is irreplaceable, but we all know that life goes on. When Og's agent asked, "who can I ever find to replace Og?" I quickly turned and said, "Lou Tartaglia." You will see why.

They both love to inspire others to reach their greatness. I knew the hardships and struggles my husband went through before he made it. I know of the personal

struggles his younger protégé has experienced. Their life experiences have given them the compassion to understand others.

Og loved Lou; they talked on the phone often, but they talked more about life than writing. You will see his deep understanding in this book. It is a story about discovering your purpose in life and the need to work with a mentor. How fitting that the mentor for the story was Og. You may even see Og's handiwork in the *Last Gift of the Magi*. He encouraged Lou to build the foundation for a sequel.

Part of Dr. Tartaglia's eulogy for my husband was that "Og Mandino was a Magnificent friend." My husband was truly a magnificent friend to so many. It is a great pleasure to present our friend to you. Enjoy "the Camel". As Og said, "This special tale is destined to become a classic that will touch lives for many decades. I salute the author."

— Bette Mandino

Contents

	Notes of Historical Interest	6
	Foreword	7
	Prologue	11
1	North of Baghdad	13
2	Caesarea Maritima	25
3	The Caravan Begins	31
4	Westward Towards Palmyra	41
5	Nazareth	51
6	Bedouin Bandits	55
7	Jerusalem, Day of Atonement	63
8	A Rendezvous with Melchior	73
9	Leaving Nazareth	91
10	The Jordan River at Jericho	109
11	The Little Town of Bethlehem	121
12	Entering Jerusalem	131
13	The Caravan Arrives in Bethlehem	149
14	The Messiach Command	157
15	The Rejection of Jamil	183
16	South to Beersheba	191
17	The Chase Begins	199
18	Storm in the Negev	215
19	The Holy Innocents	233
20	The Last Gift Received	241
	Epilogue: A Camel's Purpose	251
	About the Author	254

Prologue

According to Western oral tradition, there were three Wise Men, or Magi, who visited Bethlehem some two thousand years ago. Three was the number used for the Wise Men and was selected by Emperor Constantine's wife in the 4th Century. She thought three Magi were more in keeping with the Triune God. The original Latin records gave the names of nine Magi. In Eastern tradition, however, there were twelve. While the number of Magi may have been a point of contention between the East and West for centuries, what was agreed upon was that gifts of a special nature were brought by a caravan for the Divine Child.

Many have traveled on that caravan. This is the story of one of them, a little camel named Jamil. It is also the story of the last gift of the Magi; a story that has been lost for two thousand years. If you had visited with the Magi in the little town of Bethlehem that cold winter's morn, you would have felt spiritually blessed and somehow chosen. Your life would have changed forever. This story is being told to help you experience that blessing. The last gift of the Magi is still being given today, and every day. When you discover who is giving it, you will have met one of the Magi and behold the Divine Child.

Let the journey begin.

Matthew 2:2 . . .
"Where is the newborn King of the Jews?
We have observed his star at its rising and have come to
pay him homage."

1

NORTH OF BAGHDAD: IN A DESERT SOMEWHERE

They roughly shoved a drink in Jamil's face, and he was grateful. He had been running all afternoon, racing the other camels, and having the time of his life. Jamil was the smallest adult male at the oasis, but he wasn't going to let the bigger beasts get the best of him. He was fast. He was as fast as the shooting star emblazoned on his forehead.

Because he was so young, Jamil was allowed to run, to burn off energy. The larger camels each thought that they could outrun him and tried. But they were soon surprised to be left in his dust. Jamil was rambunctious by nature; part of that was his youth and inexperience. The rest was his personality. He liked to be right. He liked to win, and he didn't like to be told what to do. Eventually, he hoped to become a racing camel, living the life of luxury, stabled near a dromodrome or racetrack. For now, however, he had to settle on staying where his new owner brought him.

I love to drink. It is my nature, he thought, as the cool gulps moved down his throat. Yet he doubted himself and looked around at the other camels. Even though Jamil was small and young, he was very handsome. He had a gorgeous blaze on his forehead that everyone loved to touch. He looked in the water and his reflection reminded him he was as fast as that shooting star on his forehead.

Jamil gulped more of the sweet, cool water that was before him. He was thirsty because he had spent the day racing through the desert and hadn't stopped to drink.

Today, I proved that they can't make fun of my size. I'm faster than them. I showed them, he said to himself. Jamil was mumbling as he drank. He had beaten all of them back to the oasis. His heart was pounding. He listened to the noise it made in his chest. His thumping heart often sounded like a soft voice. When he raced, he imagined that voice was cheering him on.

He listened, but now it sounded like a gnawing thought that kept creeping back into his consciousness, *Experience greatness . . . camel . . . stop drinking . . . caravan journey*. The thought echoed and then faded out with his heartbeat. *You must journey through the desert and abstain from drinking in order to understand your life's purpose*. There was a part of him that felt a wisp of joy and then slowly saddened as the voice dwindled within him.

"What nonsense," Jamil muttered. "A caravan? I love the oasis and comfort. I know I am a camel and according to the elder camels, I am supposed to live in the desert, but I'm going to the city and race. I'm going to live the good life. I'm not going to be a dumb pack animal like the rest of them struggling to find the next oasis." He looked around to see if anyone noticed that he was talking to himself.

When traveling through the desert, it was vital to know the location of an oasis. During the day, the desert was hot as the sun's rays beat down on the arid plains and scorched the dunes. When night fell, however, the temperature dropped by as much as fifty degrees and chilled one to the bones. Only special creatures could adapt to

the brutal environment. No one chose to go out into the desert without an important purpose.

The oasis where this camel was drinking was known as Kashan, after the family of that name. There was always considerable activity at an oasis, and this evening was no exception. A thin crescent of moon hung on the horizon on this dark night. Everyone was talking about the strange phenomenon that was occurring in the sky near it. A new, rather bright star had appeared in the West. It had the appearance of a large shooting star that was slowly moving westward. The western portion of the star was blunted, and its tail gave it the impression of flying towards the west. It always seemed to be moving.

The usual nomads were there because Kashan was a watering spot for their herds. They were all part of the same tribe or extended family, some close, some distant, but all related by blood. Many of them had the same features with thick beards and muscular bodies. Tonight, however, the oasis was buzzing with travelers from many lands beyond Persia who were following the star.

There were elders tonight. That made it a special night. To look at them was to be fascinated, but to hear their stories was to be enchanted by the love of God. All listened attentively to the elders speak of the meaning of this new celestial body. They were speaking about how it reflected God's love for man.

These elders were Zoroastrians, followers of Zarathustra, and known as Magi, or priests, because of their status. One from the group, a certain Gaspar, was a Magus from far-off India. He was said to be a direct descendant of Sem, the son of Noah. He was the oldest of the group and

had a long, flowing white beard. He was dressed in an elegant white and purple silk garment and a purple turban. He wore a large star sapphire ring on his left hand.

Jamil tried to squeeze in to hear what was being said.

"Move away, weakling," one of the camels said. He was large and smelly and not too friendly.

He nudged Jamil aside and one of his friends moved in. Jamil had to stay off to the periphery. He was behind four older camels who were long-time friends, reunited at the oasis. Coming to a watering site was cause for celebration for camels. These four were happy to be back in each other's company. They were large pack animals for a group of men who were listening intently to the magus. Gaspar was talking about the reason the heavens had created this new star. The Zoroastrian Magi were considered astrologers, but they were more than that. They were spiritually adept and felt a responsibility to view the stars with respect. They believed God whispered his love for all His creation through the stars.

Gaspar spoke in a deep, vibrant voice that filled the cool night air. He shook his head from side to side when he wanted acknowledgment, as was the custom in his Indian culture.

"Every soul on earth has a counterpart in the heavens. Each star represents a being. We Zoroastrians believe that there is a heavenly part of each complete being. When an individual is born, the parts are separate, and at death, the individual unites with his heavenly counterpart. A new star of this magnitude represents the arrival on the earth of a special soul."

Gaspar paused and then with great emphasis spoke

deliberately, "This star is so bright and so unusual that we believe it fulfills the ancient prophecy of the coming of the Jewish Messiah." Gaspar looked around at his colleagues and moved his head to the side as they raised their eyes in acknowledgment.

Gaspar paused, waiting for the murmur that rose from the group of nomads to settle down. None of these nomads were Jewish. Some may have had Zoroastrian roots, but all of them knew that the Jewish God, Yahweh, was powerful. They knew the stories of the Israelites' flight from Egypt, the parting of the Red Sea, and the fall of Jericho, and understood the power of Yahweh indeed!

Jamil was marginally able to understand any of this. He was a young camel, not given to listening to humans and their discussions. His focus was on fun. He had a future somewhere other than with caravan drivers.

Before this, Jamil's days had been filled with running and playing. He was as carefree as the wind and until men had come and separated him from his family, his life was ideal. His parents had told him it was time for him to grow up and learn about work and responsibility. It was time to discover what it was to be a camel. They told him to listen to and obey the camel drivers.

"Carry your burdens well, Jamil," his father had told him.

Jamil was not interested in carrying burdens; he was too small, and he was a race camel at heart.

"Show respect and pay attention to your handlers," his mother said. She knew that this was going to be a problem. Paying attention was not one of his strengths, and respect, suffice it to say that Jamil had a talent for testing authority.

Jamil had been a handful for his handlers thus far. He figured being temperamental was part of being a racer. He was hell-bent on living up to that ideal.

Jamil was led away from his family by a kindly camel driver who knew the small animal was not fit for racing. He did not have the right lines or body type. Racing camels were leaner, taller, and had longer strides. At best, he would amount to a small pack animal who would only be able to carry insignificant loads. He would not bring much money, but if trained well, someone would want him. His camel driver thought he would be fit for a female rider once he matured a bit.

Jamil was young and fit, but not accustomed to working. As the camel driver led him away, he looked back fearing that his parents were right and that his life was changed forever. A few minutes later, they were far behind him and no amount of looking back could find them.

Since then, he had not paid as much attention to the camel drivers and took every opportunity to run free. When they were at campsites, Jamil generally ignored humans. They were bossy and arrogant. They could not walk or run very fast and some of them had odors that offended his sensitive camel nose. He was fortunate that the camel drivers let him run and play. They let him do this because he was a young camel and young camels always returned to the oasis. Because of his speed, Jamil always returned first.

Jamil tried to ignore humans, but tonight was different. He was listening with all the others. What was being said was extremely important. There was an air of excitement and anticipation about this conversation. It was as if a

secret was being shared. He liked secrets but didn't often hear any. His childhood had been filled with few friends and few shared secrets.

Gaspar pointed toward the heavens with both arms raised as he spoke again. "Notice the brilliance of the new celestial body. The heavens are celebrating the arrival of a grand new spirit with a powerful burst of light."

Men and camels both looked up. Jamil saw the star, too. The star on my forehead is bigger than that, he thought.

"Every year, the Magi have prayed in a cave at the Mountain of Victories, awaiting the fulfillment of the prophecy of the Oracle of Hystapes," Gaspar said.

The name Hystapes sent whispers through the crowd. For centuries, the Magi had awaited the fulfillment of this prophecy. Lore had it that the oracle at Hystapes had uncovered a scroll during a voyage over Mount Ararat. The scroll dated back to the time of the Great Flood, and it carried a list of instructions that Noah had given to his three sons. Among the list of detailed observances was the Messiach command, to keep sacred the twenty-third of July as a day of prayer and meditation in a dark cave. The purpose of the dark cave was twofold: to seclude an area away from disturbances, and to allow enough darkness so that the great light could be observed in an unmistakable way. Through time, the ritual developed into a Magean tradition. The Zoroastrians had chosen the Mount of Victories as the perennial site.

Jamil was intrigued by the legend of the oracle.

One of the older camels, who was kind to Jamil, turned and said, "Humans have so many mysterious traditions."

Jamil agreed. "They tell stories for hours on end."

Gaspar went on with his story.

"We have traveled for almost half a year since the feast day last July. I have come hundreds of miles from the northern provinces of India. I plan to meet two other groups of Magi in a short time. We will be traveling in a caravan of twelve and need some able-bodied, God-fearing men who are brave enough to travel across the Persian desert to the Roman kingdom of Judea. The pay will be good, but the journey will be fraught with inconveniences. The real reward will be that each of you who journey with us will be able to pay homage to the newborn king. You will be present at the mystery ritual of the Messiach command of Noah."

Again, a murmur went up from the crowd. This was more than most of the men were willing to bargain for. Long journeys were usually undertaken only for financial gain, not for opportunities to pay homage to newborn kings.

Jamil decided to lie down while he listened. This promised to be a long night of discussion. As befit a camel, he first got down on his knees. Other than humans, the only creature in the animal kingdom that knelt before going to sleep and upon arising was the camel.

"What kind of place is Judea?" asked Abdul, a serious young Bedouin who called no place home and yet was at home almost anywhere.

Gaspar thought for a moment. He stroked his thick white beard.

"Judea is a strange land indeed. It was given by God to the Jewish tribes so they could have a land of their own. They are a headstrong lot, and their land has been taken from them many times. The region is now under the control of the great Caesar Augustus, as he is called. It is

under the Syrian Legate Quinctilius Varus and is administered by Herod, the Governor. The land is fertile, and the hills abound with a rich harvest. The vineyards and orchards rival those of my sweet India, which I might add, is the most fertile in all of creation. Trade through Judea is very prosperous. Its safety is guaranteed by the powerful Roman legions. Laws are strictly enforced, but foreigners are treated with respect."

Abdul had another question, and he was not timid about asking.

"How long will we be traveling? I need to know the entire length of our journey. My wife is with child again, and though she is just starting the gravid period, she demands that I attend at the end; perchance a son is born to me this time."

The others laughed, knowing that he already had two daughters. He wanted to be present at the birth of this child in case a son was born. For Bedouins, having a son was crucial. One's family name would have continuity. A son could support a family. The more sons one had, the more prosperous one was. In old age, however, a daughter would be special support to a father. He was grateful that he had two daughters.

Gaspar picked up his knife and started drawing in the sand.

"We will first journey to Aleppo and then meet the others in about one cycle of the moon from there. In a fortnight, we will arrive at Palmyra and travel on through Jericho, where we will ford the Jordan River. We must present ourselves to the court of Herod, then travel a few miles south to the site where we have estimated the child

is being nursed. Our plan, at this time, is to take the same route on our return. It should take us less than four lunar cycles to arrive back at this oasis."

While Gaspar paused, a voice rang out.

"But go on Abdul!" cried his great friend Nemir. "Your woman can well have a son without you being in attendance, like a midwife. Being around for the birth of your child won't turn him into a boy."

The men all started to laugh. Nemir was well known for his ability to defuse the loudest argument with his wit and whimsical remarks. He was short, squat, and rotund. Nemir had an abundance, if not an excess, of energy. He was blessed with a sunny, endearing nature, unlike that of sober Abdul, who always wanted the facts.

Jamil watched the two men and knew they were great friends. He wondered what it would be like to have a friend with whom one could trust and laugh.

"How can so much noise come out of such a little package? It must be empty like a drum," said Abdul.

He reached out and petted Nemir on the head, obviously making fun of how short his friend was.

Just then, Jamil was nudged by another camel, who whispered into his ear, "Stop drinking . . . experience greatness . . . caravan journey."

Jamil shuddered with fear when he heard his own thoughts whispered to him.

Luke 2:1
"It happened that at this time Caesar Augustus issued a decree that a census should be made of the whole inhabited world."

2

Caesarea Maritima

The High Priest Matthias slowly walked up the steps of Herod's palace in Caesarea Maritima. The glistening limestone stood in beautiful contrast to the soft blue of the Mediterranean Sea. The polished white stone was matched only by the white of the sails of the ships in the busy harbor.

Matthias knew that Herod the Great was a "friend" of Augustus Caesar. He was no friend to the Jewish people. Matthias stopped at the top of the stairs leading to the courtyard. Roman guards looked him over, amused by the robes that signified he was a high priest of the Jewish people.

They know who I am and yet they still make me wait before they announce me, he thought.

"Your name and your business, sir?" the legionnaire asked.

"Matthias, a high priest of the Jewish people, responding to a summons by the Governor, Herod," he said dutifully.

Matthias' voice couldn't mask what he felt for Herod. He deliberately did not use the title King given to Herod by Augustus. King was what Herod considered himself. He was not the King of the Jews, except in the eyes of Augustus and the Roman legionnaires stationed in Judea.

The soldier smiled at the irritation in Matthias' voice.

"One moment, sir," the soldier said.

The legionnaire kept a straight face. Roman soldiers were good at that. Their discipline was strict. The guard was formal, but required to be polite to anyone of higher rank.

After a brief delay in which one of the other soldiers entered a room across the courtyard and then returned, Matthias was granted access. He walked across the marble courtyard with a fountain in the center and paused to look at the statue of some Roman god. It was an effrontery to his Jewish religion. Matthias entered the reception room of the Roman sub-legate.

He thinks he's the king of the Jews, appointed by Caesar, but not by God. He is expanding the Great Temple to prove he is as great a king as Solomon.

Matthias knew he needed to calm down before he entered the room. He stopped just inside the portis or Roman door. Along with the usual entourage of slave servants and scribes, were two men with Herod. One of them was well known to him, Yael, Son of Ellemus. He was a member of the tribe of Levi but was not a friend of Matthias. Yael means strength of God, but in dialect it is slang for strong as a goat. The other man appeared to be Roman.

"High Priest Matthias of the Levites," announced the inner guard.

Herod nodded for him to come forward.

"Governor Herod," Matthias said with a smile.

He, too, knew how to feign politeness.

"Matthias, old friend. I am so glad that you have come."

Herod's tone was condescending. If there was any gladness, it was because he was going to put the High

Priest on the spot. Herod never passed up an opportunity to make someone else look bad.

Matthias nodded. He preferred to get on with it.

"You are well acquainted with Yael, am I correct? He brings a Roman diplomat to us."

Matthias nodded. Herod motioned to the other man, the Roman.

"I'd like to present to you Quinctilius Varus' representative, Fillipus Varus."

Matthias let the man's last name sink in. Varus was the legate of Syria, powerful and politically astute. He had sent his son to bring a message to Herod. It was a sign that there was something in it for the legate's family and that he should be cautious.

Varus stood up to greet the High Priest.

"I bring a message from Caesar Augustus. He has issued a tax throughout the Empire to pay for Rome's armies."

"A tax? How much?" Matthias asked. He was shocked by the man's abrupt manner.

Varus did not like being interrupted.

"It is one-half percent of the value of each citizen's properties."

"One-half percent! That's ... "

Matthias knew Herod wanted him to lose his calm and react, but Matthias held his temper.

"And how does the great Caesar propose to collect a tax on the property from the Jewish people?"

It was an affront to the Jews to tax their lands. This was a land that was given to them by Yahweh. The nation of Israel was divided into regions, and Herod presided over them for the time being. There was a deeper divide in the

Jewish nation. It was a political split between the Zealots and Pharisees. The Pharisees cooperated with Rome. The Zealots wanted freedom for their people and autonomy for the land of Israel. To the Zealots, it was a grave sin for the Roman Emperor to tax a Jew. It was worse to tax the land that was God's gift to them. It reinforced the repugnant idea that they were now possessions of the Roman Empire. This was tantamount to being forced to pay homage to a false god, the Emperor. A tax on property would be repugnant to the Pharisees, too.

Herod knew this, and yet he did not defend the Jewish position.

He simply said, "A census is to be taken in each city, town, and village."

"How can you possibly tax land and possessions with a simple census? Every five years, Rome takes a census, and it is the same story over and over again. We are a nation of tribes. Our people do not keep allegiance to their city like the Romans do. We are not proud of being from Jerusalem or Capernum. We are members of the tribe of Levi, the tribe of Judah, or one of the other tribes. As a Jew, you should know that."

Herod did know that, but Matthias was referring to the fact that Herod was a recent convert to Judaism and did not see himself as a member of any tribe.

"How can you expect our people to comply with this census? All the records of our citizens are organized by family. Each family member would have to return to the town of origin of his family. Are you prepared for the chaos that will ensue?"

Herod was prepared for these questions. He knew that

a man from the house of David, for instance, living with his family anywhere in the province, would have to travel to Bethlehem to be counted because that was David's town. It meant travel and hardship for hundreds of thousands.

"There is no fast and easy way to conduct this census," Herod admitted.

"That is why the Jewish people will be given more time to be counted. My father has petitioned Caesar Augustus to give the Israelites until the end of this year to comply," said Varus. He was smug, the entitled child of a powerful politician.

"And I suppose you expect me to announce this in the Temple?" Matthias said.

There was no way that Matthias would do this. Herod knew this, and he wasn't a fool.

"No, I don't. In fact, I expect Yael, Son of Ellemus, to be declared High Priest for a day. He will then make the announcement."

"And if I won't allow it?" Matthias asked.

Herod's face clouded with a sardonic smile.

"You will have to think about how unwise that would be." He turned to Yael. "What day would be the best? We need a day when the Great Temple is overflowing with people."

"The Day of Atonement is coming. The crowds will be huge," Yael suggested.

Judges 18:5
They said to him, "Consult God, that we may know whether the journey we are making will lead to success."

3

THE CARAVAN BEGINS

Jamil got to his knees in order to stand up. It had been a long night. He looked at the older camel, searching her face for some sign as to who this was.

"I am called Heba," the older camel said.

Jamil stared at her. She was much older than his mother, but she had that same kind of warm look.

"Are you a teacher or something?"

"Yes, something like that."

"So, you were listening to the Magi. Are you going on this adventure?" Jamil asked.

"Wrong question. You need to ask if *you* should be going on this adventure. I've made long trips many times," Heba said.

"Oh, so should I be going on this adventure?" Jamil asked.

Heba smiled. She said nothing, which made Jamil feel nervous.

"I could go. It wouldn't be too hard for me. I'd get a little bored, that's all."

"So, you wouldn't have a problem if you go?"

"Hey, I look small, but I'm fast and a lot stronger than you think. I wouldn't have a problem," said Jamil.

He wasn't serious about going. He thought the trip would be decided by whoever became his handler. After a moment's thought, he decided he didn't want to go.

He knew he would have to make one of these trips in the future, but not just yet.

Heba looked him over. She had penetrating eyes.

"For years, you have lived at one oasis or another, exercising, getting faster, but never developing your full potential. For years, there has been a gnawing feeling at the core of your being that something was wrong, that you should not stay at the oasis, but you should leave and join a caravan."

"How do you know this about me?"

"Let me finish. Somehow, you understand that by facing the desert and learning to live without the constant reassurance of drink, you will discover your greatness. I am here to guide you and to answer the questions that will assault you as you face this most difficult, yet natural task."

Jamil felt like she had just reached into his heart and read his deepest secrets. His head was reeling. He wanted to run, yet he was glued there, waiting, knowing that he was in the right place. It was his destiny to be at this oasis and next to this old camel.

"I'm not afraid to go, but I think I'll pass on this one."

Being cute came easy for him because of his size. The truth was that he was afraid of being relegated to the ranks of a pack animal, and a small insignificant one at that.

"The Magus Gaspar will soon ask for volunteers. A number of men will join the caravan. Gaspar himself will come over and start to choose the animals that he wants on the caravan with him. He will make a fuss about finding a young camel who is small yet very strong, and rather fast. This Magus is looking for a camel who has not suffered the ravages of the

desert. He is also looking for a beautiful, magnificent animal with a starburst blaze on his forehead. Gaspar will admire several of the camels, and then he will choose you."

As an afterthought, Heba added, "He will bring me along."

"Yeah, so how does he know he should pick me and take you along, too?"

"This Magus is very wise. He was given this mission by God and is being led by boundless inner wisdom."

"I'm not interested."

"Your handler will sell you to him. He'll want you."

"Why would he want me with all the other camels out here? I've never been to the desert, and I don't know whether I can tolerate being in a caravan. I'm not that disciplined. I'd much rather just hang out. I'm just barely full grown, and I'm smaller than all the others. I eat a lot, too."

She smiled at his effort.

"He'll want you."

"But why me?" asked Jamil.

"Sometimes we don't know the answer to 'why me?'" said the older camel. "Even if we never learn why, we must go on. You will see, Jamil, that he will call us by our names. Trust me."

"How do I know I can trust you? It's Heba, right?"

He wasn't good with names and, more often than not, was embarrassed to ask.

"Yes, it's Heba, and you can trust me. You'll understand the significance of my name later when we get to Judea."

"Have you ever been to this place, Judea?" asked Jamil.

"No, but I have been on many caravans, and it does not disturb me to travel that far."

"Travel that far?" said Jamil. "Are you kidding? You're talking about at least three, maybe four lunar cycles. I am barely used to one day in the desert. Not that I couldn't handle it mind you, but no, I think I'll stay here at the oasis. If I kick up a storm or spit at a few people, they'll let me stay. Nobody likes a camel that spits."

Heba looked at him and smiled.

"Spit if you will, but this Magean Prince Gaspar is wise enough to know that a good camel has spunk and the ability to assert itself. He will see you as a young camel with the strength and energy that needs to be channeled. He will see a magnificent young spirit that requires a bit of taming."

"He'll see very little if I spit in his eye."

Jamil was looking for a way out. He did not want to be in the caravan, and he did not want to be chosen to carry any special load. He looked at the other camels as they got down on their knees and got unpacked. The burdens they carried were enormous. It was a lot of work, and he was definitely not interested in it. He had plans. He had his own dreams.

* * *

Nemir and Abdul walked with Gaspar. They examined the animals and talked with some of the men. Nemir kept everyone entertained with his constant banter. The Magus from India looked at the group of four and said, "Who owns this pack? They seem to be together like a family."

An old camel driver and his friend approached.

"They are ours, and we have driven them on caravans together in the past. They work well with each other."

Gaspar gave them a nod. They walked on, negotiating

with some of the other men. Nemir chatted and Abdul discussed the fees and reported to the Magus. When they came to Heba, Abdul mentioned to Gaspar that she was a particularly fast camel. She had raced in the past.

"She looks a little old," Gaspar said.

"Then she is probably wise," said Nemir.

Gaspar smiled at his quick reply. He gave a nod and Heba was chosen.

The Magus stopped walking, put up his hand, and looked at Jamil.

"Well, Nemir, why haven't you shown me this animal before? What a beautiful specimen. He is young and strong with handsome features and has just reached adulthood. Look at his forehead. The mark is like the star of Hystapes, a beautiful specimen indeed."

With that, Jamil spat at him. The Magus Gaspar stepped back laughing, wiping his eyes.

"And spirited, too! This animal will come with us."

He went over and slapped Jamil on his side.

"Good stock, a little small," he said. "He looks very strong for his size. Is he fast?"

The owner stepped forward. "Extremely fast, sire. I was going to sell him for a race animal, but he doesn't look the part. He is not tall enough."

"We'll pay you full value as a racing camel," said Gaspar.

Jamil tensed his muscles and moved his head like a racing camel ready to start. He liked playing the part.

"Now, this is what I like, spirited, fast, and he looks like he's ready to go. I will call him Jamil, after my favorite servant."

Gaspar turned to one of his aides. Whispering, he instructed him to put together a special package, a strange sort of bundle, consisting of three bedrolls tied together on a wooden frame. They brought it over and attached it to the animal.

Jamil looked at it wearily. *Why were they putting this dumb contraption on me?*

The frame extended to the other side of his hump, where it held two decorated porcelain pots for yogurt. The men who were working on it seemed to be taking extreme care, as though it was to be a special gift. It was covered with embroidered cloth, much too fine to be used for a pack on a camel's back roll. On one side of the frame were gold clasps that fastened across the tops of the beautiful yogurt pots. In the center was the most comfortable-looking, soft-cushioned seat. This was truly a unique device.

Jamil felt the weight of the bundle as he shifted uneasily from side to side. It was light. He nudged Heba, who looked at him as if to say, "Be patient, young one."

One of the men stepped back and looked at the device, then made some adjustments.

Meanwhile, Gaspar looked on and appeared pleased with what he saw. The man who adjusted the device was satisfied as well. He called in another man, apparently a tailor of some sort, who adjusted the fabric on Jamil's left side, where the device held what looked like a basket. Toward the front were two holes in the bottom that were large enough for an egg to slide through.

The basket was lined with beautiful white silk, intricately embroidered, white on white. On the outside was a carefully tufted burgundy silk overlay with a border of

white. On top, there were two straps made of satin that had been doubly reinforced.

Even though the empty pots on the right were heavier than the basket, the contraption fit perfectly over Jamil's back hump. The craftsmen hovered around the top of it, made some adjustments, and it slipped down further. They lifted it off, brought in an exquisite carpet, and laid it over his hump. They refitted the device, made some minor adjustments, and stepped back.

Gaspar was extremely pleased.

"Notice how well your rug fits," he said to the tailor.

"I made it to your exact specifications, Sir," said the tailor.

Those specifications were given to me by the Light, thought Gaspar.

"You have completed your task, tailor. This is a job well done," said Gaspar. He walked on with Nemir and Abdul to choose more animals.

The workers started talking among themselves about who would be leaving the next day. They were going to head westward on a route that would eventually lead them to Palmyra, where they would rendezvous with the last of the caravans. Word had arrived that Balthasar of Persia had already organized his caravan and was awaiting departure. The two priests, Balthasar and Gaspar, would leave after a brief meeting in the morning.

* * *

Jamil still had the contraption on him.

"Hey, little boy. All dressed up pretty, aren't you?" said one of the larger pack animals.

"I guess that's about all the weight he's fit to carry," said another, who was still smarting from a race with the little fellow.

"Great big bodies and very little brains," said Jamil.

"Oh, so you're a genius compared to the rest of us?" a brute asked.

"Leave the little guy alone. He's probably tired from carrying that thing," said Massius. He was a large pack animal who didn't think much of the brute.

Jamil swung his head to the side and clipped one of the larger camels in the head. It stung, but it shocked the bigger animal.

"Hey, watch out. He wants to fight."

"Enough. The humans will come back and punish the larger animals," Heba said. It was all they needed to hear to stop their antics.

"I'm not afraid," said Jamil.

"I know," said Heba. She saw the men coming back to take the contraption off Jamil. When they did, the teasing stopped.

"Westward leading, still proceeding, following yonder star."

4
WESTWARD TOWARD PALMYRA

The sun was barely an orange glow awakening behind the vast expanse of desert, yet the oasis was bustling with activity. Over the horizon came another small caravan containing eight camels. There were four elegant men in the caravan with at least one servant each. In the lead, on a magnificent animal, was Balthasar, Chief Zoroastrian Priest of Persia.

Balthasar had come to Baghdad from Babylonia. He had been at the Feast of the Oracle of Hystapes and was returning to rendezvous with Gaspar. They had not seen each other since they were together in the cave on the Mountain of Victories.

Traveling with Balthasar were Akreho, Arbakchest, and Astonkakodon, all Magean priests. Balthasar, however, was also a prince. Legend had it that his family was so wealthy that they had built a tower and studded it with jewels. His innate spirituality had delighted great teachers from the time he was a young child. He was famous for his wisdom. Balthasar was a spiritual leader in the land that once encompassed ancient Babylonia, and he taught with a wise and benevolent hand. Perhaps more renowned than his wisdom was his mercy. He was carrying on the splendid tradition of the Magean princes.

As the caravan approached the oasis, Gaspar's caravan silently formed up and started to march off into the desert.

They moved quietly together. Camels did not make much noise in the sand. The men were subdued out of respect for their dignified leaders. Gaspar's caravan contained nine camels and four gentlemen. Badadilma, Horsed, and Larradad, each a Magi and each with a servant. The Magi rode splendid animals.

Tethered to Heba, Gaspar's pack animal, was young Jamil. He was outfitted so elegantly that he was difficult to recognize. Over his rear hump was the beautiful Indian carpet. On top of that rested the frame with gold metal clasps holding the two porcelain yogurt pots on one side, and on the other was a basket covered with silk and satin. The majestic seat in front looked like a soft throne.

Jamil pulled on the tether. He moved sideways into Massius, who gave him a dirty look.

"What do I do now?" he asked Heba. "What's going to happen to us? We're walking off into the desert. This is a long trip."

Jamil didn't know how to keep a formation or walk in rhythm with others.

The older camel spoke softly, "Trust, young one, that we will be taken on the shortest and safest route to Palmyra."

"Yeah, but is there anything I should know before we get started?" asked Jamil.

"Today you need only take one step at a time. Feel the sand under your feet, and notice how it gives. Notice how, when the wind blows, your eyelids are protected from the stinging sand. All you must do is follow and stay near me. I will lead the way. I will be an example you can follow."

Jamil gave her a look like, "Whatever."

* * *

Life on a caravan was simple. Most of the time, the men were quiet in a meditative, pensive state. The camels occasionally bayed to each other. Once the caravan was underway, however, it took on a life of its own, winding through the desert and over the endless sands. Stray dogs, who lived on the edge of the desert, watched as the camels moved beyond their hunting range. Jamil stayed alert. Dogs were dangerous. He could outrun them, but the other camels could not.

The caravan was coming into a strange place that had piqued the curiosity of humanity for thousands of years. It was a peculiar area of the desert that looked like the landscape of another world. Few animals could live here. Life was most unwelcome. Hardy lizards and some very clever insects survived in this barren and beautiful landscape.

Jamil hung his head down and watched his large feet step on the fine sand that had been blown in from Arabia in the south. It was rough terrain, but the caravan was passing over soft sand. *How strange. My steps are soft even though the terrain is harsh.*

Scattered about were giant black stones, fifteen or twenty yards high, standing like silent, frozen animals in the desert. Sometimes the mysterious stones looked ready to move. Other times they appeared stuck, frustrated by their inability to leave the spot where they had been strewn.

"Legend has it, Jamil, that this area was once as fertile as the lands farther to the east and south. Then one day stones rained from the sky, and God refused to pour any more rain into the area. It became a desert," said Heba.

"We might get rained on by stones, little guy. You better watch out," Massius said.

"Like I really believe it," Jamil retorted.

"I think they're beautiful," said Heba.

"If you ask me, they give me the creeps. They look alive. Watch out! That one just moved!" Jamil warned.

Heba ignored his antics.

They had traveled only a few hours, but Jamil was already tired of marching. He longed to break into a run and was acting up.

Massius did not ignore the antics.

"What's the matter, Jamil? Is the fancy little throne too heavy for you? They are probably going to have you carry a little princess around in circles when we get there."

Jamil bristled. He spat at Massius. He had great aim.

The two camels butted heads a couple of times as they were walking.

"You know, I'm carrying gold. It's an important gift. You'll probably wind up as a Roman circus camel or perhaps used for children's birthday parties."

Massius kept it up.

Nemir watched the two animals and pulled Jamil back before they ran into each other again and the contraption was damaged.

"This little one wants to fight with that pack animal, Abdul."

"He's got spunk. Keep him back for a while."

The two leaders, Gaspar and Balthasar, noticed the animosity and nodded to Nemir that he was doing the right thing. They rode in the front, discussing philosophy and charting their course with their knowledge of the stars.

They did not want to be interrupted by camels spitting at each other.

Jamil was bored. He would rather be up next to Massius and continue to spit at him. At least he could have some fun. It annoyed him to be part of the caravan. He longed to be back at the oasis sprinting with his friends, or somewhere else, at some other time, just not here. He was angry. When his temper seethed, he needed to run, not patiently walk a path with others toward a Divine Child. He would have loved to be racing Massius the beast. *I'd kick so much sand in his face that the blockhead wouldn't be able to see where he was going.*

Heba knew what he was going through. That is why she would love to race when she was younger. There was a certain maturity that developed while traveling in a caravan.

"I know the feeling of frustration and that need to run," she said.

Jamil looked at her. He was too angry to talk.

Heba continued, "I used to spit when angry and work myself into a frenzy before a race. Finally, they sold me off to a man who took me on a long journey to the tip of the Arabian Peninsula. On the caravan, I learned to focus and pace myself. I was a better racer after that."

"I'm out of rhythm with everyone else. It's a pain in the neck," said Jamil.

"That's because you are smaller."

Jamil bristled. He was waiting to be insulted.

"You'll get into a rhythm if you just keep marching and keep your mind in the present," she said.

"It's too easy. That's the problem," Jamil said. He drifted

into the future, uncertain and unsure of himself. His dreams seemed derailed by his fate.

"Stay focused on the now. Just take it one step at a time. Once the rhythm takes over, it will become effortless for you to walk across the desert. It will become part of your nature, and you'll feel the flow."

"Yeah, I'm going to flow all right. I'm going to flow right into the sand!" cried Jamil. "I'm taking one step at a time, and it seems as though it's going to take an eternity to get there. If they let me, I could run like the wind and get there in half the time."

"I'm sure you could. It's hard for one as young as you to learn to pace yourself."

"It's boring. It's never-ending. Been there, done that. I can't believe I'm involved in such drudgery," the younger camel exclaimed.

The older camel laughed.

"It's drudgery until you make it your own, until it becomes a part of you. Then every time you take that first step off into the desert, you are filled with joy."

"Happy, happy, joy, joy!" he said with each step.

"So now you're filled with joy? Good!" Heba teased back.

Jamil wasn't buying this.

"Filled with joy? I'm filled with dread that I have to do this forever. I was always afraid of this. For the rest of my life, this is what I am going to be. I'll be tied to another camel, walking in a caravan over the hot sands, unable to drink. Walking one step at a time, sometimes for two or three weeks at a time."

"You will learn things of such value to you that it will be a joy, not drudgery, to walk over the desert."

"I've got this rhythm down already. So, what's this cadence called?"

Jamil was right. He was walking, smooth as silk.

"Oh, I remember the name of this rhythm. It's called boring."

Jamil continued to mumble. He had an irritable side to him that he liked to show. His toughness was a veneer over a spirit that needed to feel important. He wanted to become a camel in the truest sense of the word, able to cross great stretches of barren desert, yet he did not want to be on this caravan or involved in it in any way.

* * *

A few more hours passed. It seemed like an eternity for the young camel. More hours, and always the same thing. One step at a time, over and over. No joy, just sand under the feet and these silly rocks in the way everywhere... ever moving on westward toward Palmyra, one step closer to some goal that he did not understand. Meanwhile, Nemir and Abdul kept him separated from the larger camels.

Frustrated, Jamil again began to complain to Heba.

"Why did I have to be born a camel? I think I would have preferred to be a cow, or a goat, or a sheep, or maybe even a human. Well not a human, they're strange. But why do I have to be an animal that spends its time in the desert without water? You do know that the sun tends to make animals hot and thirsty?"

"Good questions. They have been asked by many a

camel when he leaves his family to go into the world on his own," said Heba.

She wasn't going to feed into Jamil's drama.

"Why do I become who I'm supposed to be by living without water? This is a special talent given to me by God? It seems silly to me. I would much rather be something or someone else."

Heba just looked back patiently. She waited for him to settle down.

"You know, you look rather handsome in that new outfit. I think the role becomes you. You just don't see it yet."

Jamil kept his mouth shut. The load he was carrying was beautiful. He had to admit that. It wasn't Gold, Frankincense, or Myrrh, like some of the others. But why complain? No matter how much he complained, he got the same response: how fortunate he was to be on the caravan, how fortunate he was to be in the desert, and how fortunate he was to be chosen to carry this silly yogurt contraption.

He couldn't wait for nightfall. At least then he would be able to sleep and not have to endure this constant drudgery. Maybe he would finally get some rest. He yawned.

"I'm so bored. Maybe I could teach myself how to sleepwalk."

Heba smiled. She loved his huge, overactive imagination.

Isaiah 11:1
"A shoot will spring from the stock of Jesse;
a new shoot will grow from his roots.
On him will rest the spirit of Yahweh ... "

5

NAZARETH

Mary's smile was radiant. *She is glowing*, thought Joseph. Like any other husband and soon-to-be father, he could see the joy in her countenance. Simply radiant.

Mary looked up at him and smiled again. He could see that she enjoyed his affection. He was a kind man, with an even disposition, by nature. He rarely worried, but as her belly increased in size, his attentiveness increased too.

"It will be a boy and you will name him Jesus," the angel had said. Joseph wondered about the old wives' tale that a woman with a boy had finer skin and looked even more beautiful when pregnant. She was a beautiful young woman with perfect features. And to think I almost divorced her.

Mary was radiant and filled with joy. She was carrying the joy of the world in her womb. Joseph and Mary privately believed this child would be the Messiah. Only Mary's cousin, Elizabeth, was in on the secret.

Joseph was a carpenter by trade. He had strong arms, a strong back, and a fine work ethic. He was also good-hearted to his friends. He was finished for the day and was preparing to go out to his small shed to work on a cradle for the baby. There were still a few months until the baby was due, but he was not a man to put off work until later when he could get it done now. Besides, he was building

something for his boy. Just thinking about that was enough to fill his heart with love.

Joseph had one small doubt about the coming child. They were living in Nazareth. According to scripture, however, the Messiah was to be born in Bethlehem, the town of David, not Nazareth. Was the prophet Micah wrong? Other things made sense. It was Isaiah who said that the Messiah would be born of a virgin and out of the house of David, according to Samuel. Mary was a virgin and I am of the house of David.

"Bethlehem?" he muttered as he stepped outside.

Mary heard it and smiled. She had complete faith and knew what he was thinking. Even though they had no plans of moving to Bethlehem, she knew the message from the Angel Gabriel was true.

Joseph knew it too. He just could not figure out how to make that happen. He let the thought go as he made his way to the shed. He had saved to buy special wood for the cradle. It was cut from the fine cedars of Sinai. The smell of it in his shop was delightful. This was a labor of love. His little boy was coming in the next few months, and he wanted Him to have a carpenter's work of art for His cradle.

Joseph picked up the first cedar board and checked it for straightness, as he had been taught. It was a carpenter's habit, even for a piece that was going to be bent and curved by his skilled hands.

"Measure twice, cut once," he said. He remembered the simple lessons that his father had taught him long ago.

A boy . . . One day, I will teach him how to measure and cut. He will know how to drive a nail straight and true into a fine piece of wood. I will show him how to make a dovetail,

a tongue and groove, and box joints, just like my father taught me. A smile crossed his face. It was a father's good old-fashioned earthly pride for a coming heavenly prince.

Isaiah 40:31
"They that hope in the LORD will renew their strength;
they will soar as with eagles' wings;
they will run, and not grow weary; walk,
and not grow faint."

6

BEDOUIN BANDITS

Jamil looked at the strangely beautiful new star that lit the darkening sky. I'm tired. We have to stop to rest soon. Jamil's hopes were immediately dashed.

Balthasar and Gaspar increased the pace of the caravan. Jamil heard the wild dogs barking off in the distance. The camel drivers exchanged nervous glances at each other. Heba was silent, as were the other camels, but Jamil knew something was up. Even Massius was tense. The muscles on his powerful neck and shoulders were twitching nervously.

Suddenly, from the top of a large sand dune, three camels appeared. The riders were dressed in black, making them much harder to see on the horizon. It was an unusual dress for the desert, but it was nighttime. A moment later, they disappeared behind the dune, and the caravans picked up their pace even more.

"Who were those men?" asked Jamil. He was running at an easy pace, keeping abreast of Heba and the others.

"They are Bedouin bandits," she said.

"Which means?"

"Evil men who live in the desert waiting to prey upon caravans. We'll be all right. They look for smaller caravans than this, small groups that they can attack to steal their goods."

"What do we do if we are attacked by bandits, Balthasar?" asked Gaspar.

"We don't have swords, so we must outrun them first

and use our whips and slings. If we don't drive them off, someone will be killed," said Balthasar.

Abdul came forward.

"May I speak, sir?" he asked.

"Are you concerned about the Bedouins?"

"Sir, we are not well armed. The camel drivers only have whips. How shall we defend ourselves?"

"We come in peace. God will protect us."

"I understand, but they will attack."

"They can't possibly hope to succeed. There are too many of us."

"No, sir. They intend to separate a camel or two from the caravan and run off with them," said Abdul. He was a man of experience. He knew the ploys of these bandits.

"I see. Do you have any suggestions?" Gaspar asked.

"Yes, Sire. I think we should move the pack animals to the center and keep the strongest men on the ends of the caravan."

Gaspar turned to his personal assistant and said, "Go ahead. Tell the men to be ready for an attack. They may defend themselves with their whips, but be careful. We will hope to outrun them."

The men reorganized the caravan, moving the larger and more powerful animals to the outside.

Jamil was in the middle, toward the rear of the caravan. Heba was to his left, on the outside. Massius was to his right. The camel drivers slowed the pace down a bit as they prepared themselves.

Suddenly, from over the top of a large sand dune to their south, came the three bandits. They were yelling and waving their swords.

The entire caravan picked up speed while the camel drivers, with their whips ready, took a position near the rear.

The bandits continued to yell. They rode up alongside the caravan, swords brandished. On a prearranged signal, they drove their camels into the center of the caravan, causing them to break into two groups. The whips of the camel drivers were ineffective in their efforts to protect the ends of the two smaller groups.

Abdul, who had a sling, whirled stones through the air, missing twice, but causing the men to duck. His third stone hit his mark, striking the man in the back of the head. The bandit stopped to attend to his wounded head. Whips lashed out. He was pulled off his mount as the caravan drove on around him.

The two remaining bandits managed to separate three camels from the caravan, Massius, the large pack animal carrying gifts from Gaspar, Heba, and young Jamil. The gold latches on the side containers on the little camel convinced them that he was carrying precious cargo. Now they focused on trying to separate Jamil from the others. They were keen on gaining the contents of the contraption. If there was more daylight, they would have seen that it was empty.

"Turn away from the dune," yelled one of Gaspar's drivers.

Heba and Massius heard and followed his command at once. Jamil slowed down. He dropped back. The others moved away from the Bedouins, but Jamil hesitated.

"Take off Massius. Stay with Heba. I can outrun these fools."

Jamel was completely separated from the other two. He made a break for it, but turned in the opposite direction. He ran swiftly, but the Bedouin bandits stayed in hot pursuit. They had their eyes on his apparatus and its gold. The buckles alone were worth their bother, but they were sure there was more. This had to be the treasure chest.

"He used himself as bait to save the two of us," said Massius. He suddenly had a different view of the bantam camel.

"Jamil knows what he's doing," Heba said. She smiled, knowing what was coming.

* * *

The Magi slowed the caravan down, allowing the two camels to catch up. They watched helplessly as Jamil dashed away from the bandits, who were still in hot pursuit.

"We are going to lose our little camel, I fear," said Abdul.

The Magi said nothing.

"Where will they get another camel and device?" asked Nemir.

They watched as Jamil ran further away, with the two bandits screaming behind him. They came to a long, tall dune and the little camel ran right up to the top. He stopped and looked back calmly at the wicked men chasing him. The sky was dark. The bandits were two evil shadows, darker than the night. The entire caravan watched Jamil's lighter silhouette against the starry sky.

"He stopped. Is he fatigued?" said Gaspar, watching from the distance.

They were almost upon him when Jamil lowered his head

and started running again. The gap between the young camel and his pursuers suddenly lengthened.

The wounded bandit remounted his camel and started off in pursuit of Jamil. He had the angle on Jamil. The bandit bore down on the young camel, but Jamil ran relentlessly.

"If the other bandit gets in front of our little one, he is doomed," said Nemir.

"Look at him run. He is as swift as the wind," yelled Abdul. He waved his fist in the air in encouragement.

* * *

Something deep in Jamil sang a song of delight. He was running again after so many days. He loved to run. The wind was in his face and his hoofs pounded the sand. He was kicking up his own private sandstorm behind him. He slowed down again to let them catch up so he could spray them with sand. As the dark figures got closer, the little camel ran more swiftly.

"Come on fools! Follow me," Jamil said.

He was taunting the other camels, letting them get closer and then pulling ahead. He was playing with them and all the while watching to make sure that Heba and Massius, the pack animals, were back in the safety of the caravan.

Jamil spotted the third bandit coming at him from an angle. He was going to be cut off if he turned back towards the caravan. He smiled and turned toward the third Bedouin, closing the distance and making it easier for him to be cut off.

"Come on, you old fool. Chase me," Jamil shouted.

The last camel was as evil as its rider and poured on the

speed, thinking he would soon catch Jamil. He was hell-bent on punishing the young beast.

As he came closer, Jamil said, "Now let me show you what I have in reserve."

Jamil reached down and from some hidden place within his racing camel heart, he pulled out at blinding speed. It was as though he flew. When the other camel saw this, he slowed down in defeat, despite the whipping he was receiving from his rider.

* * *

"He has the wings of an eagle, this one. He grows not weary, he flies. He has outrun two camels so far. Come on little fellow, find the strength," said Balthasar.

The camel drivers watched in rapt attention as the race wore on. Finally, with a burst of speed, Jamil pulled away from the last bandit. It looked effortless.

The drivers, and even the Magi, cheered.

"Now, will he find his way back to us?" said Gaspar.

"If he turns this way, we shall send two men back to retrieve him. If not, he will continue to run and get further away. With his remarkable speed, we will never catch him."

They watched and waited.

* * *

"I made it. I out-distanced those guys. I knew I could," said Jamil.

There was deep satisfaction in his voice. He was alone, however, and needed to find the caravan. He couldn't see them outlined against the sand. I need their help. Some things are best done in a group. Crossing the desert was

one of them. This was a huge admission for this stubborn little beast.

Jamil continued to run, now at half speed, cooling down, getting further away from the bandits, who had given up in frustration. To his left, he heard the barking of desert dogs and veered away from them. He was running towards the caravan at an easy pace. A short while later, Nemir and Abdul tethered him and brought him back to the caravan. They hitched him to Heba. Massius was next to her.

"I am so glad that's over," said Jamil.

"You're very fast," said Heba.

"I've never seen anything like it," said Massius. There was respect in the huge camel's voice. "You deliberately had them chase you."

"I knew I was fast, but I didn't know I could run that fast until I had to."

"You are perhaps even swifter than I was."

"Maybe one day I could race," said Jamil.

"The things we discover about ourselves when we are put to the test are the things that we need to fulfill our destiny," said Massius.

"Well, I need a rest and some water. And I need to get off this caravan if I'm ever going to use my talents."

Jamil thought about racing. It was the ultimate life of luxury for a camel. Its rewards were the best feed, the finest stables, and adulation. The bonus was that you got to run as fast as you wanted.

Lev 16:34
*"And this shall be an everlasting statute unto you,
to make an atonement for the children of Israel
for all their sins once a year."*

7

JERUSALEM
DAY OF ATONEMENT

Matthias awoke after sunrise. He was sweating, angry, and late. He dreamt that he had made love to his wife. The dream was vivid. It was so real that he was not sure what happened. Perhaps he had made love? He was angry because of what that meant for him. The Jewish custom forbade him from presiding over the temple as its High Priest on the day that he had been intimate with his wife. That made him even angrier. Why Lord? Why today of all days?

Today was the Day of Atonement for the Jewish people. There would be tens of thousands of pilgrims at the temple. Other priests could perform the ceremony as the High Priest. Many of the priests were Matthias' very close friends. It was important politically to pick the right man. His first choice was Zechariah. He was older and quite popular among the zealots. Other names flooded his mind. As Matthias sorted through the men who could take his place, it suddenly dawned on him that it was going to be Yael, son of Ellemus, just as Herod had planned.

Matthias dreaded that. He rushed to get dressed. He needed to get to the Temple as quickly as possible. He had to stop it. There was a short meeting of the Sanhedrin this morning and there he would have to announce that he could not perform the ritual animal sacrifices because of his unclean state.

I will take some teasing about this.

He had to make certain that someone acceptable was appointed. He already had convinced his friends on the council not to allow Yael bar Ellemus to be the High Priest on the day of Atonement, as Herod had demanded. After much arm twisting, they agreed, but insisted that Matthias be the High Priest. He accepted. He had planned to refuse to read the announcement of the census because it violated the sanctity of the day, but Yael would.

Matthias was late. He rushed through morning prayers and almost ran out of the house, leaving his family to wonder why he was running.

A few minutes later, he walked into the South Door to the Temple and rushed up the steps. He ran across the great courtyard.

I'm getting too old for this sort of thing.

He entered the meeting room and stopped, out of breath and frantic.

"Ah, Matthias. We are glad you are here," said one of the Sanhedrin. He moved out of the way to let the High Priest step through and take his seat.

"I must, regrettably, pass today, and abstain for the next twenty-four hours by law."

The men immediately understood and smiled.

"Couldn't wait until tomorrow, old man?" one of his friends chuckled.

"He is still a young man at heart," said another.

Matthias did not smile back. He scanned the room for the politically appropriate person to take his place. Zechariah was not there. His absence was probably due to John, the young baby his wife Elizabeth had a few months back. He had to find someone else.

"What about the request from Herod Antipas to have Yael, Son of Ellemus, be High Priest for the day?" a colleague asked.

"You can't deny the Governor's request now," said another.

Most of the men on the Sanhedrin were nodding in agreement. It was as though they had completely forgotten about the census proclamation. Matthias looked around the room. His eyes were pleading for them not to do it. He knew what was coming.

The vote was quick and final. It was politically motivated. Even though many of the men in the room did not like Herod, they liked to curry favor with power.

Yael stood to address the Sanhedrin. It was short and simple.

"Thank you for the honor." He smiled at Matthias.

* * *

A few hours into the day, the crowds had grown considerably larger. There were tables set up along the huge inside walls that stretched ten to fifteen blocks. Vendors were selling doves, sheep, and calves. Blood sacrifice was done with ritual exactness, but the sheer magnitude of the crowds made it a mind-boggling logistical nightmare.

Herod entered the Temple into the expansive Court of the Gentiles.

Many of the Jews stopped talking even though he was only in what was the huge outer courtyard standing on Solomon's porch.

Herod's attendants brought a perfectly fatted calf.

A young boy asked, "Who is that man?"

"That's Herod, the Roman Governor of our God-given lands," the child's father said.

A neighbor caught the man's sarcasm and nodded in agreement.

Yael, High Priest for the day, came out of the Inner Sanctum. He walked across the Courtyard of the Gentiles to Solomon's porch.

"And that is the High Priest. He is going to take the calf from the Governor. Then he will sacrifice it on behalf of the Roman Emperor," the father explained.

Caesar Augustus had learned from his uncle Julius Caesar to be tolerant of the local religions in his Empire. This made the Roman lands easier to govern. In Judea, there was a daily gift sent to the Jewish sanctuary and a daily offering in Caesar Augustus' name. Today though, it was a beautiful fatted calf that Herod took to Yael.

The offering of the gift was pompous, but it made for good public relations. It was also coming at a price, for it was time for the announcement. Herod handed the decree to the High Priest.

Yael took the parchment and held it open for a scribe to see. The scribe had a loud voice, and it was his job to make announcements.

"We have a communication from Caesar Augustus," the scribe announced.

He waited until the crowd quieted and then looked over the first line. He paused and handed it back to the High Priest.

"I can't read that."

"It's in Latin, Aramaic, and Hebrew. You will read it three times," said the priest sternly.

"Read it yourself, Yael," Herod said.

The Governor's face had a sour expression. It was a prelude to losing his temper. Herod was not a man to disobey when he was on the brink of losing his temper.

The custom of the Roman Empire was that a mandate would be read in Latin first. Yael read it in Latin and some in the crowd understood. When it was read in Aramaic, the local language, there was considerable anger in the crowd.

"How dare they tax our lands!" an old man said.

"It is blasphemy! It violates our commandments!" said a zealot. He was furious.

"It is not blasphemy," said the High Priest.

Yael read the proclamation in Hebrew. It sounded like an insult in Hebrew, and the High Priest knew it. He wanted to take the calf and seek refuge in the sanctuary.

"These Romans worship pagan gods and now they want to tax the land that God Himself has given us. Rome shows no respect to God almighty."

The crowd murmured its agreement.

"One-half percent is outrageous!" people were yelling.

"It pays for peace," said Herod.

"It pays for war in Rome's provinces. They will eventually make war on us," said an old man.

"Rome has been tolerant to us," said Herod.

"How?" yelled someone many rows back.

"They have allowed freedom of religion. Jews are not summoned to our tribunals on the Sabbath. When we distribute food to the poor on the Sabbath, we allow Jews their portion the next day," said Herod.

"You distribute on the Sabbath!"

It was not lost on anyone that Herod was speaking like a Roman and not like a Jew.

The High Priest interrupted, "Caesar has allowed us to collect money for the Temple. Our sacred books are respected."

"Herod speaks like a Roman, not like a Jew!" someone yelled.

Herod scanned the crowd for the man. He was furious.

"He wasn't born to a Jewish mother," another said.

The crowd got quiet. They knew this was stepping over the line by talking about things no one could talk about, at least not in public. Herod was part of a group that had converted to Judaism, but no one dared insult him like this. His mother had converted, so technically he was born to a Jewish mother. He was still considered a second-class Jew in the eyes of many.

Herod looked at a centurion standing on the porch of Solomon and nodded.

Matthias saw the makings of a riot. Roman soldiers would not be kind. He stepped forward. It had a calming effect on the crowd.

"How does Caesar propose to collect a property tax?" Matthias asked.

"It's simple, a census," Herod started.

"You mean impossible. The Roman census proceeds town by town. Our property is not registered by town!"

"We register our property and our holdings by family, not by geography. Our records are kept in the Synagogues of origin," said Matthias. He was trying to keep the crowd calm by presenting the obvious objections to the tax.

"Rome knows that and respects it."

Herod was a bit calmer and under the false impression that Matthias was helping him.

"Roman tax collectors will assess each citizen's holdings from the family ledgers. There will not be a tax on each citizen, just his property."

The problem with that was it was a tax on God's gift to the Jewish tribes.

"Each citizen will be required to return to the city where his family is registered and declare his holdings."

"You mean, I have to travel all the way to Beersheba?" a man yelled out. His irritation was matched by his contempt.

Herod turned to look at who it was. The crowd closed in around him and he was hidden.

"There is no way you can expect this to happen. It is a hardship for families. It means travel and chaos," Matthias said.

"You will have extra time to comply, but before the other side of the year shows its face, it will be done," Herod said.

It was a veiled reference to Janus, the Roman god for whom the month of January was named. Janus had two faces, one that looked back, and the other that looked forward. It was an insult to the Jewish people to hear references to the Roman Calendar and the Roman god Janus in the Great Temple of Solomon. They had their own calendar.

Herod turned on his heels and left.

* * *

Mary heard about the census in the marketplace.

People were angry. She heard a zealot say, "One day, a Messiah will come and free us from this tyranny."

She made her purchases and rushed home. She went immediately into the shop to tell Joseph.

"Mary, is something wrong?" he asked.

"I just came from the market, and everyone is talking about a new Roman tax. They are going to tax property."

"How do they propose to do that?"

"A census and we will have to travel to Bethlehem."

"How interesting. If it was later, when the baby is due, we would have an excuse to travel to Bethlehem."

They knew the prophecies better than most. The scriptures referred to Mary and to the Child she was carrying in her womb.

"It would look strange for us to go down there and then travel again when he is due."

"They are saying that we will have until the start of the new year, according to the Roman calendar. Don't you see, Joseph? We can wait until the baby is almost ready, and then we will go to Bethlehem for the census."

"Your kinsfolk will think it foolish to wait so long," he said.

"Yes, perhaps, they will. However, if we wait just the right amount of time, we will be there, and it will be too late to travel back. He will be born in Bethlehem and fulfill the scriptures."

"The Messiah will be born from the house of David. But you, Bethlehem, though you are small among the clans of Judah, out of you will come for me one who will be ruler over Israel, whose origins are from of old, from ancient times," Joseph quoted the prophet Micah.

Matthew 2:10
"They were overjoyed at seeing the star."

8

A RENDEZVOUS WITH MELCHIOR

For nearly five weeks they traveled westward, following the star. Each night, the Magean priests discussed the phase of the moon and the positions of the stars. The clear nights and shining stars revealed many wonders. The men who had come along gradually became immersed in the process that was unfolding. The days were long because they often did not stop for camp until it was quite dark. They liked to follow the star in the early evening when it was more visible.

Jamil was not enjoying any of it. The entire time he had been trudging through the desert, he kept hoping that something exciting would happen again. All that happened was that on occasion, the other camels would tease him about his yogurt pots. Trudging along, drudgery, and ridicule were not what he was made for. His mind continued to wander.

There was barking off in the distance. It pulled his focus back to the here and now. Everyone on the caravan heard it, too. Jamil watched the furtive glances of the camel drivers. Some were worried. The more experienced men nodded gravely, but remained confident.

The barking sounded closer and Jamil began to worry that the stray dogs were back.

The last couple of days, as they traveled farther west, the land had become progressively more fertile. There were packs of dogs following the caravan. They generally

kept their distance, but if they attacked, it could be dangerous.

The oases were closer together, and the heat seemed a little more bearable now, but his attitude had not changed. He decried his fate to be born a camel and become a pack animal. The camel drivers, moreover, were hardly merciful, pushing their animals to get the most out of them. The older camels were used to this treatment. He wanted to be as tough as them, but resented being driven. He especially resented being driven into the evening. *Evening was the time for relaxation; it was time for nature to rest. It was time for play*, he thought. He moved from animal to animal, looking for someone to romp or run with. They all wanted rest.

This was an important night. They were to rendezvous with Melchior near the city of Palmyra. Centuries-old Palmyra was a great city that was involved in extensive trade with both the East and the West. It was part of a route that stretched far east, across the Persian territories to India. It was a prosperous area where agriculture and grazing sustained the populace. With the advent of increasing trade from the East, its people had become wealthy. In recent times, it had come under the dominion of Roman law. Syria now had a legate named Quinctilius Varus, who was of senatorial rank. That meant that Varus had friends in high places. He ruled with the typical iron fist of the empire. Roman order had enhanced Palmyra's already productive trade by guaranteeing that commerce could be carried on without danger.

News that another caravan was arriving already had reached Palmyra. Many people in the city were interested,

having already welcomed Melchior from Arabia. They were looking forward to the arrival of two more princes and their caravans. Melchior had met the Legate and had a cordial but brief visit.

Gaspar and Balthasar, however, had decided that they would make camp on the outskirts of town. They tried to avoid any contact with the general public. They did not wish to inconvenience or force hospitality from the rulers of the areas they traveled through. It was difficult for a caravan of princes to not draw the attention of the local rulers. The Magi did not want to create fear or jealousy. Varus had met Melchior, and that was enough.

The short and very blunt Nemir enjoyed teasing his tall, thin friend, Abdul. They were near the rear of the caravan where Heba and Jamil were stationed today. For much of the trip, Jamil had been forced to ride directly behind Heba, near Gaspar and Melchior, but today they rode toward the back. Abdul and Nemir were with them. The two men were so different on their camels. One swayed back and forth, tall and thin, and the other was firm and short in the saddle.

"I've always wanted to come to Palmyra," Nemir said. "There are probably a lot of places you'd like to visit, Abdul, but you never seem to get around to it."

"There are a lot of things I can see when I ride that you miss," Abdul said.

"I've told you before, it's a big world out there."

"Thank God, you dragged me along on this caravan so I will get to see a little of the world," Abdul retorted.

"A fine nomad you are! You never left the area where you were born."

Abdul chuckled at his friend's teasing. He watched his short, wide friend barely rock from side to side.

"It is to my advantage that I am so squat. My head doesn't move from side to side like yours when you ride your camel," said Nemir.

"If it did, we would most likely hear a loose rattle."

They continued to banter for a few minutes. The two men lived in adjacent villages along the Tigris River and had been on many trips together. Abdul did not travel as often as Nemir because he raised camels. He called it "Dromedary Husbandry" and took it very seriously,

Abdul looked at the contraption on Jamil's back.

"What do you think this thing is for? It will certainly hold yogurt because they said that those are yogurt pots on that side. But this other thing to the left is kind of odd. You can't put anything in it because there are two holes in the bottom."

Nemir looked back at it again.

"Have you noticed how the camel is carrying it now?" he asked. "He has the cadence down to exactly the right speed. When he walks, it doesn't jostle from side to side."

Abdul thought about it for a while.

"I've observed how smooth he is. The contraption is very stable, even though it is not filled with yogurt and there is nothing in the other basket. But you may also notice that they keep adjusting the speed he moves at. Occasionally, Gaspar looks back to watch it and makes us walk faster, then slower. Sometimes, they even run him at the end of the day."

"Yes, the old men watch him closely when he runs . . . and the beast loves to run. Have you ever seen a camel so fast?"

"No, but they aren't testing him for speed. I've raised a camel or two and watched how they test speed. No. They watch how he does with the contraption. You've noticed that too?"

Nemir chuckled. "I thought that's what was going on, but I don't see the reason for it."

"I think I understand why," Abdul said. "Whatever they're going to carry in that left side must be very precious. They are trying to train the camel to walk or run without shaking it. They are teaching the camel to walk in a rhythm, very still and very peacefully."

"I have an idea," Nemir said. There was a twinkle in his eye, hinting that he was going to say something silly. "I think that they're probably going to have a contest when we arrive at this newborn prince. They will put eggs in that basket to see which camel can walk most carefully with the eggs. Whenever one falls out, the camel loses."

Abdul frowned. He was such a serious type.

"Oh, please. They are going to carry something that cannot be shaken too much. What it is, I do not know," said Abdul.

"It could be a rare wine, something that must not be agitated," said Nemir.

When Abdul frowned again, Nemir added, "You have any better ideas?"

"Jamil is well trained. Notice his gait. There is something regal about it. He is stronger because of the training. When he runs, he is the fastest camel I've ever seen. He is as smooth as liquid on polished marble," Abdul said.

Nemir paused and leaned closer to whisper.

"Did they tell you why they asked you to fill it with sand today?"

"No. They made me fill each yogurt pot with sand and then wrap a large stone with cloth and lay it in the other basket. He is now moving even smoother."

The beasts were listening. Jamil was paying closer attention than the others.

"Interesting questions . . . what are Magi priests doing with that little basket, Jamil?"

"I don't know, Heba. I've listened to the same stories every day. I am bored. I'm tired of trudging along. How much longer do we have to go?"

Young camels often asked if they were there yet. Older camels ignored the question. They knew that it was the journey and not the destination that honed one's character.

"But you still wonder about this little contraption, don't you?" asked Heba.

"It could be worse," Massius said. His new friend was carrying a tremendous load.

"The weight isn't bad. I'm not having trouble carrying it. But why this thing? They keep marching us at different speeds so that the basket doesn't sway. I understand that. I can feel the difference. In fact, I kind of like the feeling of everything being balanced on top of me. I learned to carry this thing right away. I learn quickly. I'm ready for anything," said Jamil.

"But, my friend, you do grow weary," said Heba.

Heba was playing with him. She was waiting for him to complain again. He easily took the bait.

"I am weary because nothing happens. The whole thing seems stupid. I've been wondering about the purpose of caravans too. Is it to carry packages and goods across

open spaces, for the benefit of man? It makes some sense to be of service and to do that work, but here I am on a caravan carrying something whose..."

Jamil could not find the right word.

"... utility is unknown to you. It is far less useful than some of the gifts you've heard them talk about bringing this young child," said Heba.

Jamil wanted to carry Gold, Frankincense, or Myrrh, something of great value like the others. He wanted to feel important.

"Even though I can do this brilliantly, and I do carry it brilliantly, I'm not suited for this work. I've been given a delightfully temperamental character. If I had different qualities, like patience or understanding..."

"Ah, Jamil," said Heba. "You have the qualities that are necessary to fulfill your appointed task. The problem is that we don't always understand the task given to us in life. We are usually given two simple alternatives," said Heba.

"You mean like do it and shut up or don't do it and suffer the consequences?"

Jamil had seen the nastiness of some of the camel drivers when an animal refused to follow orders. The Magi frowned upon it, but it happened when the animals and men were tired and frustrated.

"One is to do whatever your current duty is to the best of your ability. Enjoy it as well as you can. Trust that there is some force controlling your destiny. This force will use what you have done for the benefit of man," said Heba.

"Or don't do it." *I love finishing her sentences*, he thought.

Heba smiled at him, and Jamil wished he had her patience.

"Or you can continue to oppose it and ask 'why?' and try to discover a way of escaping the task that stands before you. You can rationalize and justify why you should not do it. Behind that attitude is a belief that if you do not take care of yourself, no one else will."

"That seems true enough for me," he said.

"Because you believe that there is no higher intelligence which could direct your life in a way that would benefit you and mankind."

He thought she was finished, but before he could make a rebuttal, she started up again.

"The desert is a wondrous place. It is filled with life forms often hidden from our eyes. It is a system of such delicate design that even the scorching sun and hot winds are perfectly balanced to keep it alive. It is bustling with life."

She motioned for him to look around.

"See the little lizards scurrying about? Every nook and cranny of the desert has a creature in it. Many of these creatures cannot be seen with the eye, yet their life affects yours in unknown ways. This force, the Sustainer of life, is active always, but more so in the desert, where life is very fragile and conditions are precarious. Reality is harsh, Jamil. Extremes of temperature exist. Resources are limited and must be utilized most effectively. Here, the Sustainer, as we camels call Him, gives us the ability to operate and survive in conditions that, for most animals, would cause death. He gives us the ability to survive in the hot sun, in strong winds, and in sandstorms that would grind away the hides of other animals. There is stability required to survive in such a cruel environment."

Jamil knew she was right. That stability was God Himself, directing every living creature in the Universe. Jamil did not mind most of the conditions. He didn't like to admit it, but he was suited for it. Sometimes the harshness felt good, even invigorating.

"Our task is to let the Sustainer work through us so that we may discover ourselves and be true to our camel nature. We leave the oasis and the freedom to eat and drink as much as we want. Then we march off into the barren wilderness and allow what the Sustainer has placed within us to manifest its glorious self."

She finally paused. She hoped it would sink in. He hoped she had stopped for a while.

"You make it sound so wonderful. Yet, when I look around at the reality of what we've come through - weeks of marching on the desert sand, pushing westward, focusing one step at a time - it doesn't have the same meaning to me as it does to you. You talk about what we do, this banal effort, this one step at a time, as though it were a glorious miracle unfolding before us."

"Ah, but it is, Jamil. It is the miracle of discovering your true nature. The Sustainer has bestowed within you the power to accomplish this task. He has given you enormous resources you have yet to tap. He has given you the capacity to live fully in an environment that would wreak havoc on most living organisms. But he has also given you the task of learning about yourself to live your life to the fullest."

He thought about what he had learned. So far, he had discovered that he could run faster than even he had dreamed. He discovered that he could survive on a caravan, even though it was boring at times. He didn't need to

eat or drink like other animals, and he survived just fine. There was something else, though. He knew intuitively that he hadn't tapped into it yet. The thought excited him. He wondered what it was.

* * *

The two Magi had reached the outskirts of Palmyra and the caravan came to a slow halt. Balthasar and Gaspar pointed out a location where they wished to settle for the night. In the morning, they would rendezvous with Melchior, the third of the great Magi. From there, the caravan would prepare for the journey to the Jordan River.

"Abdul, have you ever walked a camel across a large river?"

"No, Nemir, but I hear it is quite a treat."

"A treat indeed. The poor animal sees more water than it has ever seen in its entire lifetime. It can't decide whether to obey and keep walking or just stay there and play. A camel is not well suited for playing in the water and is a terrible swimmer. The first thing we do is to make sure that the camel is full and doesn't need to drink."

"I've transported my camels over the Tigress on barges. We blindfolded them rather than water them."

"You don't want a thirsty camel in the middle of a river. It starts to wander all over, trying to drink as much as it can. Then it gets crazy and throws off all its packages. Eventually, it will wander to a spot that is over its head. The poor camel is sunk," said Nemir.

"It makes him that crazy?" said Abdul.

"The more water, the crazier it gets. The more it tries to drink, the more out of control it gets. Everything that you

have worked for, that you have been carrying for such a long time, gets lost in the river."

"I've heard stories about that, about caravans being lost, because they weren't properly prepared to cross a river."

"It is smart to develop a support team for each camel if you are going to bring the camel through a lot of water."

"What do you think the Magi will do?" Abdul wondered.

"They will tether the younger camel, the so-called special one, between two older camels. He is much less likely to get rambunctious if he has one behind him and one in front of him when he walks through the water."

"That makes sense, especially if the water is running quickly," said Abdul.

"They say, however, that it is fairly easy to ford near Jericho. There is a point where the river is not deep. Even though the water runs rapidly, the pull on the camels' legs is lessened because it is shallow."

"If the water gets deep, it pulls on their bodies. It must have a profound effect on the camel."

"It drives them crazy, Abdul."

Balthasar motioned to Gaspar that he had sighted something off toward the north. They sent one of the men into the distance to what looked like the camp of Melchior. A few minutes later, he returned and informed them that it was indeed Melchior's camp.

As they approached the camp, a tall, rather handsome young black man slowly rose from the group of Magi. He walked out to face them. As Gaspar and Balthasar approached, the young man bowed, and with a flourish, he welcomed them as though they entered a majestic palace.

Accompanying Melchior were three other Magi: Aksherosh, Sadlak, and Merodak, who rose and stood behind him. Melchior of Arabia was the youngest of the Magi.

Balthasar, Gaspar, and Melchior had been friends for years. Theirs was not a superficial friendship. They were united through the deep bonds of the Magean priesthood. These men had a spiritual connection, since each had taken a sacred vow to carry on the Magean traditions. But there was more to it than that. It was the jovial friendship of two older men who loved Melchior like a younger son.

"Hail, Melchior," cried Balthasar. "We are now twelve priests, my good friends. Our group is complete."

Gaspar nodded. "The Messiach command will be fulfilled."

"How was your journey?" asked Melchior. He extended his hand to help the older Gaspar down from his camel.

The three leaders of the Magi discussed their voyages to the Jordan River. These were three men who represented the known races of the world. One was from the Orient, one from African roots, and the third from the cradle of civilization.

Their primary concern was fording the River at Jericho. Their secondary concern was avoiding a disturbance with their presence in Jericho. These were twelve regal gentlemen. They could not pass through a city or remain in its vicinity without being noticed. Thus far, they had been able to stave off the hospitality of the regional rulers. They knew that as their journey eventually drew to an end, they would be required to talk to the Romans. They were in the Syrian province and only Melchior had

met with the legate. Once they passed into Judea, the situation would be different. Herod the Great was a controlling and demanding man. He would try to find out everything he could about their trip.

* * *

Jericho was a large city on the other side of the river. It was the first large city in Judea. News of their arrival had preceded them. Officials from the city would try to meet them to show them hospitality when the caravan made the crossing.

The camel drivers sat talking about how they would ford the river at Jericho. Everyone had some experience, and each was willing to share it.

Melchior and Gaspar approached them, and they stopped their discussions. Gaspar introduced Melchior to the group.

"Gentlemen, this is Melchior of Arabia."

The prince of Arabia was received warmly by the camel drivers.

"As you know, gentlemen, in a couple of days it will be time for the camels to ford. Let me tell you what I have in mind for the crossing."

Melchior lifted his staff and pointed to the ground. The camel drivers moved in closer to watch.

"This is the Jordan River, and this is our encampment. We will attempt to ford at this point. The residents tell us that the river is shallow here. It is the perfect point to cross. You, gentlemen, are responsible for properly managing the camels," said Melchior.

The men nodded to each other.

"My men have been instructed to work with you, and together we should be able to make this phase of the journey a safe one. However, as you know, crossing a river with camels is not easy."

The preparations for the ford would take at least two days. The animals needed to be completely rested and calm. Some drivers believed that they needed to wait until the camels were longing to travel again before attempting a river crossing.

"I wish you good luck. And I leave you, Abraham, as my man to coordinate the crossing."

Abraham sat down with the camel drivers. They started a lively discussion as the Magi walked over to where the camels were tied up.

"Gaspar, show me the special one and the carrying device," said Melchior.

Nemir and Abdul got up to accompany them.

They walked over to Jamil. Melchior was pleased.

"A beautiful specimen indeed. A lovely animal. He is a little small, though." He touched the blaze on Jamil's forehead.

"I know, he has the star," said Gaspar. "I recognized him right away. He was the one who appeared in my dream. This beast is capable of walking and running without shaking the device at all."

"We will have to make sure that he is well protected during the crossing. We do not want to excite him," said Melchior.

"That is true. He runs like the wind, and if he gets loose, it will be hard to catch him. He likes to be near this older camel."

"Should we blindfold him?" Melchior asked.

"My handler doesn't subscribe to it. It spoils their temperament."

"Did you name him?" asked Melchior.

"Yes, Jamil, but the drivers call him Little One. He is a little rambunctious, but still young. He learns fast too."

"Is this it?" asked Melchior. He pointed to the contraption lying on the ground.

"Yes," said Gaspar.

Balthasar walked over.

"Beautiful, isn't it? Indians know how to work with fabric. I was telling Gaspar yesterday that I must send a caravan back with him to bring back silks for the ladies of my court."

Melchior knelt to feel the fabric and examine the device.

"So, this side is for yogurt or water?" he asked.

"Whichever they choose."

"And this side is for..." Melchior smiled. "I hope they like it."

"I see no reason why they would need a camel in Judea. It would be much easier for them to bring a donkey, or to purchase a horse. In any case, we are doing what we were instructed to do. We will follow our inner guidance, and things will work out for the best."

"Life is like that," said Melchior. "Carrying out the will of the Great One gives us a sense of easy participation in life, regardless of how difficult the task."

"How true," said Balthasar, and Gaspar nodded. They noticed Nemir whispering to Abdul.

"Do you think they always philosophize? Do they sit around and act like priests all the time?" Nemir asked softly.

"Nemir, quiet!" said Abdul. "These men are royalty. They can act in any way they choose. It is not our place to question it."

Gaspar glanced at Nemir. He smiled.

"You're right, we always philosophize."

The other men laughed.

Luke 2:3-4
*"And everyone went to be registered,
each to his own town. So Joseph set out from
the town of Nazareth in Galilee to
David's town called Bethlehem..."*

9

LEAVING NAZARETH

Mary and Joseph walked into the small marketplace together. She was late in her term and could not carry everything alone. Today, they were buying provisions for the trip they were going to make for the Roman Census.

Joseph's family was from Nazareth and other towns in Galilee. They belonged to the house of David, as many others in the village did. Most of his relatives had already made the trip down to Bethlehem and back. He was taking criticism from some of the cousins for putting the trip off so late into Mary's pregnancy.

Miriam, a particularly vocal cousin, stopped them in the street.

"I see you are still here, Joseph. How are you feeling, Mary?" said Miriam.

"I am well . . . " she hesitated. The baby kicked. "And the baby is well, too."

"When are you leaving?"

"Tomorrow," Joseph said. He smiled and took Mary's arm. They started to walk on, but Miriam wasn't finished yet.

"Don't you think it's a little late to travel?"

"It is the law. We don't have a choice," said Joseph.

"I didn't know you obeyed Roman law so diligently," Miriam said.

Joseph had enough. He knew he had to wait so that the child would be born in Bethlehem, but he did not need sarcasm from a nosy cousin.

"Miriam, please. I have not wanted to leave until now," said Mary.

Miriam looked at Joseph. Her look said he should be able to get his wife to go when he wanted.

Joseph and Mary walked away, secretly smiling.

"What a pain in the neck. She's been like that since she was a little girl. She loves to make you feel guilty. It is an art form for her," said Joseph.

"She has clay feet like every other human," said Mary. Her tone was filled with support for her husband.

"Clay feet? She is a woman with a clay mouth."

They both laughed.

* * *

The morning had broken late. The December sun rose in the Southeastern sky over the peak of Mt. Tabor and found Joseph had already saddled their small donkey. Mary packed provisions for the journey. She had yogurt, bread, grains, and dried meat for them to eat. Joseph loaded a water urn onto the side of their mule. It was a strong beast that was capable of carrying an enormous amount of weight, but occasionally had a temper tantrum. A carrot or some other sweet vegetable was usually enough to get him moving.

The normal three-day walk to Bethlehem was going to take possibly four days, perhaps longer, because of Mary's state. She was young and healthy, so they planned on traveling as fast and as far as she wanted each day.

If she wasn't pregnant, they would be able to go faster, but going up the mountains in Samaria was much harder carrying a baby. Joseph was a strong man and capable of keeping up with the donkey, but he wasn't sure how fast Mary could tolerate it.

Mary looked around their little house one last time. Her hands rubbed her swollen belly, comforting her soon-to-be-born baby.

"Give me strength, Father," she prayed softly.

Joseph smiled at Mary. He gently led her out of the house to the donkey. His relatives would watch the small home since most of them had already gone to register for the census.

Their donkey walked at a fairly quick pace. Joseph carried a walking staff that he would put to good use during some of the climbs. The road out of the village of Nazareth was small and rough. It passed by a fallow field that bordered the edge of the cliff on which the town was built. At the base of the cliff, it joined the road out of Sepphoris a few miles away. This road was a major thoroughfare and ran to Gabae near the coast.

Joseph led his wife down the winding Roman road through the valley of Jezreel. This was the easiest part of the journey. He kept checking on Mary. She was smiling sweetly while softly singing psalms that she had learned as a young girl at the Great Temple. She was singing the praise of the Lord to the Lord himself.

"O God, give your judgment to the king; your justice to the son of kings; That he may govern your people with justice, your oppressed, with right judgment," sang Mary.

"Psalm 72?" Joseph asked.

She nodded and continued to sing. She got to the part that said, "May the kings of Tarshish and the islands bring tribute, the kings of Arabia and Seba offer gifts."

Joseph smiled. He will be the King of kings.

Mary continued to sing while Joseph focused on the road ahead. Other travelers were going to the towns of their ancestors to register for the tax. Soon they came to the branch that led into Samaria. The road turned south, then a short distance later, started up into the mountains. Most of the travelers were heading that way because they were going to Jerusalem. They were making great time. The donkey was moving quickly and Joseph was walking at a brisk pace.

Joseph was thinking about the heavens as he looked up at the gradually rising terrain. He thought about the angel's visit. "It will be a boy and you will name him Jesus."

Mary continued to sing, "May his name be blessed forever; as long as the sun, may his name endure. May the tribes of the earth give blessings with his name; may all the nations regard him as favored. Blessed be the LORD, the God of Israel."

Joseph joined her at " . . . who alone does wonderful deeds. Blessed be his glorious name forever; may all the earth be filled with the Lord's glory."

"His name, Jesus, will be blessed forever, Mary."

"I know, my sweet husband," Mary said.

A man on horseback passed them and nodded at the couple. He was moving in haste. He would arrive quickly at his destination. The young couple did not have that luxury.

The travel was getting gradually more difficult. Mary and the little beast were doing well, but Joseph was

concerned about Mary getting too tired and not being able to make it to a town with proper accommodations. Samaria was not an area to be traveling through at night, either.

By midday, they had to stop. Mary was tired and needed the rest. Joseph was hungry. He unburdened the beast and moved the animal away toward an open area to graze. He tethered the donkey to a small tree. They had covered more than fifteen miles of the more than sixty-mile journey quickly, in just under five hours. They needed to cover another ten miles before nightfall. Their pace would be slowed in the hills.

"Joseph, would you like some bread and yogurt?"

"Yes, Mary."

He watched her spread a small blanket on the ground and then bring fruit and yogurt over. She took out a satchel of dried fruit and another with almonds. They had a variety of dried grains and a special mixture of fruits, grains, and seeds, called Daniel's blend, that Mary insisted would give him strength for the trip. It was a family recipe that had been handed down through the generations. It was not unlike the Charroset eaten at Passover but had grains and seeds added to it. Mary insisted that this was the secret mixture that sustained Daniel in days of old.

Joseph had to admit that it did give him more energy than anything else he ate. It tasted good, too.

Their midday meal was short, just as the daylight hours were. They needed to arrive in the city of Sebaste before nightfall, so Joseph loaded the donkey and then helped Mary onto the little beast. They started again. By now, there were more travelers on the Roman road through

Samaria. This was a positive for them. More travelers meant safety on the roads.

"There are so many and they move with such haste," Mary said.

"They're rushing to finish the obligation to Caesar. Many have put this off for as long as they could, but now it is almost too late."

Citizens put the registration off because of the harvest. Vines needed to be tended, grapes to be gathered and wine to be made. Fields of grain and fall fruits needed harvesting. They also put it off, however, out of resentment of Roman rule. The nearly three-month period to register for the census was supposed to avoid the massive population movement that was going on throughout Judea, Samaria, and Galilee. It hadn't worked at all. Most Jews were trying to register at the last moment to avoid paying the tax too early.

"What will we find in Bethlehem, Joseph?"

"Do you mean, when will we meet cousins?"

Mary smiled.

"Probably not. My family are now Nazarenes and Sepphoreans. My father's family moved to the Galilee region generations ago."

They passed the road that led to the small city called Sebaste by the Romans, but originally called Samaria. They pressed on. Joseph was relieved that Mary looked well. He was tired and he could see that the donkey was starting to show signs of fatigue.

* * *

Less than an hour later, they reached the village of

Lebonah. The name meant Frankincense. It was bustling with people who were journeying to Jerusalem and other destinations in compliance with Caesar Augustus' proclamation. Joseph found an inn with a vacancy and they rested for the night.

When they finished their prayers, he noticed that Mary was rubbing her stomach. The baby seemed to be lower, and she had an unusual look on her face.

"Have the pains started?" Joseph asked. There was alarm in his voice.

"No, it's just a tightening of my stomach. It has been going on for the past few days. It's a little stronger now," Mary said. She was thrilled that the birth would be soon.

"Are you sure?"

"Yes, don't worry. I'm rubbing because it feels better when I do so. Let's sleep."

* * *

When Joseph awoke, Mary was already up, rubbing her stomach again. She was singing softly to her baby. He heard the soft words of Jeremiah and smiled.

"The word of the Lord came to me, saying: Before I formed you in the womb, I knew you . . . before you were born, I dedicated you . . . a prophet to the nations I appointed you."

She looked over at Joseph.

"The Psalms are so much sweeter when I sing them to Jesus," she said.

"Have you been up for a long time?" Joseph asked.

"Just a little. The tightening got stronger, but it is less now," Mary said.

Joseph looked around the small room and realized she had prepared a modest breakfast. He quickly said his prayers, and they prepared to leave. He was worrying as any expectant father would.

Joseph had no idea how far they would get today. They wanted to make it to the road that branched to Jericho. There was a small village that was called Mizpah, less than twenty miles away. Mary's family had friends there and they would help them find a place. They would be within ten miles of Jerusalem and fifteen of Bethlehem.

The distance they needed to travel today was less than yesterday, but the terrain was rougher. Both travelers were tired. The donkey seemed fine, however. He took his burden with ease.

Joseph helped Mary into the sidesaddle and hoisted his pack and walking stick. They were off. There were empty vines in the mountainous terrain. Harvest was over and the fields were empty, yet the land was still beautiful. It was God's country, given to the tribes of Israel. This is being taxed. Joseph shook his head. He felt the loathing that every Jew knew. He accepted it as God's plan to have the prophecy of the Messiah fulfilled.

A short time later, Mary interrupted his thoughts.

"We need to stop, Joseph,"

Mary was fatigued. She had not made it nearly as long as yesterday. She looked more tired than he had ever seen her.

"Can I get you anything?" He asked

"I need a small meal and some refreshment."

They ate some oranges and shared a pomegranate.

After only a short rest, she announced that she was ready. She seemed refreshed.

She is a remarkable young woman.

By the midday hour, they were much further than he expected. They stopped again.

"I do much better with a few small meals. I have no stomach left," said Mary.

"Really?" Joseph said, smiling and looking at her large stomach.

She was rubbing her belly, and they both burst out laughing

"You know what I mean . . . no room in my stomach, silly man."

"Are you feeling okay?"

"Yes, we must press on. We must get to Bethlehem by tomorrow."

Suddenly, Joseph was worried. Her tone said that she knew something was about to happen. "We must press on because the child must be born in Bethlehem."

Out of you, Bethlehem will come one who will be ruler over Israel.

* * *

When they stopped at sunset, they were just beyond a road to Jericho and had reached the town of Mizpah. Joseph was pleased with how far they had come. They had traveled most of the distance on the so-called road to Galilee that led to the gates of Jerusalem. They were, at most, sixteen miles away from their final destination. Mary was desperately in need of rest by now. One more day of travel in her condition would be brutal. Though she was

the type that never complained, Joseph could see in her eyes that she was having a difficult time.

The family that they had hoped to stay with was not able to accommodate them. Everywhere they went there were travelers. It was as though the entire census was being completed in the last week. They barely managed to find cheap lodging somewhere else.

* * *

Meanwhile, the caravan was also at rest, awaiting the impending Jordan River crossing. Jamil looked over at Heba. "I am a little anxious about tomorrow's crossing," he said.

Heba knew that each of God's creatures faces temptation that tests its mettle. She knew tomorrow was Jamil's day of temptation.

"Go to sleep, young one," said Heba. "You will be safe."

But Jamil did not sleep well. He lay there and, in his imagination, saw water; great expanses of water, larger than he had ever dreamed of before. Inside, he felt as if he were going to go crazy. Something told him that if he tried hard enough, he could drink it all. Something inside him was not quite right.

Heba watched with a knowing eye. She understood what her young friend was going through. She understood the anxiety of not knowing one's reaction to the water, and she understood the desire to drink. She understood it as only a camel could. It was the need to take just a little more, leaving one feeling totally out of control. It was a need to take one more gulp, one more mouthful . . . a need to feel full, regardless of what lay ahead. It was a need to fill an emptiness inside, yet never feeling full.

Temptation always tried to fill an emptiness that only God could fill.

Jamil was awakened by a quartet of older camels who were gazing from the hill out over the short plain to the river. One of the four was debating whether he should make a run for it, head down to the river, and immerse himself in the flowing water. The three others convinced him not to do it. They started to ululate or wail, as camels do when struck by the desire to enter the water. The ruckus woke a few of the camel drivers who watched the antics of the four. It was the serenade of love that could neither be consummated nor relieved.

"Is that one in pain?" Jamil asked, referring to the youngest of the four. The fear in his voice was not hidden too well.

"No, he has been through this before and is grateful that his friends kept him from going in."

"They sound so sad."

"Don't let them fool you. They are having fun crying on each other's shoulders. They just want their friend to know that they understand."

* * *

Joseph knew he should sleep, but he tossed and turned, constantly checking on Mary. He knew she was pretending to sleep and trying not to wake her husband.

Finally, Joseph realized they were both trying to comfort the other by pretending to sleep.

"Are you worried, Mary?"

"No, I'm thrilled. The time has almost come. It will work out perfectly."

Her voice was soft and sweet. She could not wait to hold her baby in her arms.

"I worry about finding a place fitting for the birth of the Messiah," said Joseph.

"It will be perfect no matter what."

"But there are so many travelers. As we get closer to Jerusalem, there are fewer and fewer places open at the inns. I have never seen so many people on the road, not even for the great Feasts."

"We will find something, settle in, and get ready. I will have you at my side and my baby in my arms. It will be wonderful."

* * *

When morning came, Mary needed much more time to get ready, but not because she was tired. It was something else. She had an unusual amount of energy and was fussing to get everything just right. He watched her in amazement. She packed everything as neatly as possible.

Joseph didn't know it, but the burst of energy meant that her nesting instinct had kicked in. Her time was very near.

Joseph finished feeding their beast. The poor little donkey had not done this amount of work in a long time. He usually pulled a small carpenter's cart around Nazareth. He was ready and willing, though, and hadn't given the couple any problem. Joseph believed that the animal looked forward to carrying Mary and the unborn child. However, Joseph had to lead the animal at a slower pace because Mary was so uncomfortable. Every few steps he could see her discomfort, along with the patience and the sweet anticipation of the soon-to-be mother.

"I can see the shining city on the hill," said Mary.

It was every Jew's delight to see Jerusalem. The temple stood out at the city's highest point. Next to it was the ugly Antonia fortress being built by Herod. On the other side was the Hippodrome, but it wasn't visible from where the couple was. The tall towers of the Hasmoneam Palace were visible too, but it was the Temple that enthralled the couple. It was Jerusalem, the city named by God. Yira meant to see, and shalom meant peace. To look upon this city was to see the peace of the Lord.

Mary started to think about her parents, Ann and Joachim, and how they supported the sacred role she was destined for. They had lived near this section of the city. She wished that they were still alive. However, if they were, they would have stopped her from traveling, knowing that she was close to delivering her baby. They knew the scripture and would have known that she needed to get to Bethlehem. Mary had been promised to them by an angel. She was born to the couple when they were very old, beyond the usual childbearing age. As a three-year-old child, she was consecrated to God. The couple joyfully watched their little girl climb the steps of the great Temple, enraptured with a pure love of God. Mary had spent most of her childhood at the Temple. They knew that their daughter wanted to be close to God more than anything else.

When Mary was fourteen, the Temple maiden in charge of the young girls decided to bring her to the high priest to find a spouse for her. The High Priest, Zacharias, knew the young virgin quite well. He was her uncle and espoused to Elizabeth. He had been one of her teachers at the Temple

and knew of Mary's sanctity. The priest prayed for guidance and discerned that she should marry a man from the House of David. He had asked for eligible young men from that House to come to the temple with a branch that had a bud of a flower on it. Each man was asked to place the branch on the altar. The one whose flower opened was to be chosen.

Joseph was the only young man to show up without a branch. He went out and grabbed a thick branch from the Gethsemane gardens behind the Great Temple. His bud miraculously open when it was placed on the altar. The Priest indicated that this was God's choice for Mary.

"I wish my parents had met you," said Mary.

She felt the first strong contraction.

Joseph watched her catch her breath and then breathe out slowly. She focused on the Temple the entire time. He could tell that it was strong.

By noon, they were approaching the great gates of Galilee, which was the final destination of the road they traveled.

People were everywhere. Mary and Joseph slowed down to pick up some fruit from a merchant outside the gates. They sat for lunch off to the side and rested. It was mid-afternoon before they were ready to travel. Bethlehem was normally no more than a leisurely two-hour walk. Hopefully, they would get there before nightfall and find a place to stay. She was pondering all that had happened since that eventful day at the well months ago. *Yes, I know, born of a virgin*, she thought.

That referred to the Prophet Isaiah, who wrote, "Therefore the Lord himself will give you a sign: the virgin will

be with child and will give birth to a son, and will call him Immanuel."

Mary was visited by an angel while drawing water at a well. She conceived a child with the Holy Spirit. Mary went to visit her cousin Elizabeth, who was elderly and with child. She stayed until the birth to help out and to learn what to expect when it was her time to deliver.

When she returned a few months later, Joseph could see that she was pregnant. Her husband had not consummated the relationship, and she was still a virgin. Mary's pregnancy was of grave concern to him. It was a scandal, but only for a short time. Mary knew that Joseph could cancel the engagement.

Joseph planned to divorce her quietly. It would have been an enormous shame to everyone.

Thankfully, Joseph was visited by an angel who told him, "Take Mary home as your wife, because she has conceived by the Holy Spirit. She will give birth to a Son and you must name him Jesus."

When Mary got up and suddenly held still, the woman vendor realized her condition. Her eyes became wide.

"She's in labor, young man. You must find a place for her immediately."

"We can go into Jerusalem," Joseph said. He was speaking as a soon-to-be father. He worried about what was going to happen.

"Bethlehem," Mary whispered.

"Hurry young man. Get her to her parents or relatives. Take your wife some place safe and make her comfortable," said the merchant.

Joseph grabbed the donkey's lead and started off.

When he got right up to the gates, Mary again said, "Bethlehem. He will be born in Bethlehem. If we stop in Jerusalem, with me in this condition, they will never let me continue the trip."

Joseph knew what he had to do. He turned right at the gates. He took the road that ran past the stone quarry and ugly hill called Golgotha. He turned right again onto the road to Bethlehem. She was in labor. The contractions were coming at regular intervals.

Mark 1:5
"… and they were being baptized by him in the Jordan River, as they acknowledged their sins."

10

THE JORDAN RIVER AT JERICHO

As the morning sun rose crimson over the horizon, the camel drivers started their work. They fed and watered the animals so that they were ready for the day's events. They lined up the animals, tethered Heba in front of Jamil, Massius behind him, and started to march. After a few minutes, they reached an embankment where the entire group beheld the magnificent Jordan River. It was everything that was in a camel's dream. Though the smell of it had caressed his nostrils for some time, when Jamil finally saw the water flowing gently through the countryside, he could not believe the effect it had on him.

Surely, they wouldn't mind if I stopped and drank, Jamil heard himself think.

"Watch your thoughts, little one," Heba said softly.

"This water looks so pure, so wonderful. Surely there would be no problem if I paused in the middle and let myself drink deeply."

The river looked as though it was washing through the hills, purifying the countryside. It looked so natural, so beautiful, so gentle and friendly, but as they approached the river's edge, Jamil quivered. Something inside him was trembling, almost shaking. It was a nervousness he had felt before. It was the anticipation of something wonderful, yet fearful. He was afraid that he would lose control of himself to this intense pleasure.

The group paused at the stream. The camel drivers quickly checked the tethers between the camels, which were divided into groups of six. Each group was going to wade across at its own pace. They would wait on the other side, where their burdens could be checked and re-secured if necessary. Half of the group could return and help the drivers with their animals.

The first group of more experienced camels strode across quickly. The drivers yelled, "Wellow! Ay!" and made all sorts of noises to keep the animals distracted. The pace was brisk, but not so fast as to disturb the bundles they were carrying. The idea was to get the animals across as quickly as possible, freeing up three of the men to help the other animals journey across.

To the observer, the task of walking the animals across the water looked like a matter of course, simple and smooth. But something dreadful was happening inside Jamil. He felt a strong desire that seemed to be escalating, a feeling of temptation. The closer he got to the water, the more intense the humming or vibration within him became. As he approached the water's edge, he went from feeling excited to jittery and finally just plain fearful. *I could let myself die here and not mind a bit.*

Heba looked back.

"Are you okay, little one?" she asked.

Jamil was too stimulated to answer.

"Ah, the water's fragrance . . . It's getting to you, isn't it?" Heba asked.

"I've never seen so much. The aroma is so powerful and sweet. It's speaking to me, drawing me in."

Jamil's speech was pressured.

"Be careful, little one," said Heba. "Pay attention to what your duty is. When we enter the water, concern yourself with putting one foot in front of the other and look at the distant shore. Keep your thoughts focused on where you need to go. Do not try to control your feelings. Control where you put your feet."

"My thoughts are on the water, Heba, the water. It's everywhere. It's incredible. It's so beautiful and so peaceful."

"Just one step at a time, Jamil. One step at a time. Stay with me."

Jamil felt the tether pull as Heba was driven into the water. He also felt Massius behind him, bumping him as he started off. Jamil took his first step.

"This is incredible! I want to jump right into it and lose myself in the water. Maybe I can take a small taste. I've never seen water as pure or as fantastic as this; it must be delicious. I can't control this, Heba. I can't control what I feel. Wow!"

Heba turned her head to him.

"You don't have control over what you feel. You can only control what you choose to do. Understand that? You must take one step at a time."

"Keep walking! Stay focused on the far shore," Massius warned sternly.

Slowly, they started to move across the river. Jamil could feel the different rocks and formations under the pads on his feet. Camels' feet were great for walking in the sand, but they did not feel quite right in the water. They felt as if they were being pushed around by the flow of the river. Jamil noticed that as long as he kept his focus on

the other shore, his feelings did not overwhelm him. However, when he looked at the water, he wanted to dip his head in and drink. He immediately felt out of control.

"But, Heba, suppose we stop here in the middle, and I just knelt to feel it all over me. I want to be completely in it. Suppose I did it just this one time. I may never cross a river like this again."

"Perish the thought, Jamil. Just keep moving. Stay with me."

Jamil felt the tether get taunt and Massius bump him. The drivers yelled at him because they could sense that he was intrigued by the sensual flow of the water around his legs.

He was nearly overwhelmed as he looked at it.

Such beauty, he thought. *Such wonder. Why did the Sustainer make rivers? Why would he make a body of water this large if I wasn't supposed to jump and play in it? . . . If I couldn't lose myself in it? And why would He make it have such control over me and make me feel the way I do? Maybe the Sustainer wants me to immerse myself.*

Jamil continued to rationalize as they marched across. He felt lightheaded, but at the same time, he felt a deep dread. In some profound way, he knew that if he stopped and got into the water, he would lose a part of, or perhaps, his entire life. He would lose something that he cherished. He knew that there was no immersing himself in this pleasure without the loss of something just as important. But he wasn't sure that it would be a tragedy. As he thought about it and felt the water pull at his legs, he began to believe that there would be no tragedy at all.

Maybe just this once, it is my destiny to feel the river come up over my body and immerse myself. Maybe it is right for me to reach in and drink as much as I want or am able to.

Jamil was startled by the driver yelling at him. He felt as if he was suddenly shocked out of a dream.

"Come on, little one! Come on! Keep your head up!"

The driver put a stick under his head and kept prodding him to keep moving.

Jamil wanted to stop. He knew it was wrong, but he wanted it more than anything in the world. He wanted to kneel, even lie down in it. He wanted to join with it, become a part of it. This feeling was so powerful that his legs were getting weak. He felt the whack of Nemir's staff on his hind quarters. It was stronger than the temptation. Thankfully, it got his attention.

The pace picked up. They were more than halfway across. Jamil felt sad because he recognized just how powerless he was over water. He realized how little control he had over the instincts and emotions that welled up when he was around this source of indescribable pleasure. He was heavy-hearted because he knew that he had no control over what happened inside him when confronted with the desire to drink; even more so when confronted with the desire to immerse himself in it. He was a camel; he could not drink like an ordinary animal. He would drink and drink until there wasn't room for more. He realized that he had no control over what he would do if he were allowed to play in the river.

I have to leave the river, that it is my fate ... to continue my journey.

The sadness intensified as they approached the other shore. He felt as though he must even relinquish his right to fantasize about it because even that left him weak and out of control. It was the feeling of saying goodbye to a friend. His lot in life was to resist the temptation of this incredibly sensual pleasure.

They pulled him closer to the shore. They marched him up onto the embankment. He recognized, in the midst of his melancholy, a truth about himself.

"I am a camel, Heba. It is my nature to want to drink. Yet it is also my nature, as designed by the Sustainer, to live in the desert."

"Yes, you are. Just like me, you are out of control in the water. My entire being also becomes unmanageable in water. There is no survival, no discovery of oneself, and no living to one's full potential until I recognize that I am powerless over the water. To immerse myself in the drink is to die, but to be the camel that I am is to live."

With a sigh of relief, he stepped up onto the grass above the bank of the river. Jamil again admitted that he was powerless. But instead of being annoyed with the way the Sustainer had designed camels, a small joy slowly started to filter into his consciousness. Something inside had shifted. His view of the world had changed. His surrender to God's way had opened him up to grace. Joy was filling the hole in his soul where fear had been.

"Jamil, if I recognize who I am, if I am rigorously honest about my camel nature, with all the defects that camels have regarding water and living in the desert, I still can experience joy and peace. It may only be just for today, but you can have that too."

"She is right," said Massius. "Every time I fantasized or better yet romanced the pleasure, I would get stuck and the feelings would escalate out of control. God allows the temptation to help you understand your nature. If you don't give in, you grow stronger."

"I felt weaker."

"He means stronger in a sense of understanding yourself better," said Heba.

"I finally realized the punishment for giving in was the pleasure I received, which would eventually lead to my destruction."

Jamil welcomed the calm coming over him. It was a growing peace. Somehow, he was back in touch with another part of his camel nature. He was back in touch with a reservoir of peace somewhere inside him. It was okay to be a camel. It was okay to be out of control when he was in the river because he was not designed for that. Every fiber of his being knew this. With this realization, he grew more serene.

Three of the camel drivers stayed with the six animals. The rest went back into the river to help the next group as it waded across. Jamil turned to Heba.

"Do you think those other camels are feeling as out of control as I did?" he asked.

"Of course. It is really powerful, isn't it? After a while, you get a kind of reprieve, because the feelings grow less intense with time. Sometimes, if you pray with full humility and complete surrender to the Sustainer, the feelings will slowly vanish," Heba said.

"I've experienced that too, Jamil," said Massius. "It is grace poured upon you and it sustains you when you are feeling most powerless."

"Some of them look upset to me," Jamil said.

"Those camels are feeling it. If it happens to you again, I suggest that instead of fantasizing about immersing yourself in the depths, pray to the Sustainer to be released from its power. The Sustainer created you and can release you."

Jamil and his mentor continued to watch the other animals being driven across. He hoped . . . yet doubted . . . that he could ever have the overwhelming desire removed from him. It was not that he wished to drink or enter a river and play. He just doubted that he could live one day without his emotions becoming unmanageable. He was grateful when they turned the herd of camels around and started marching off toward the city of Jericho. He wanted to keep the river and those insane feelings behind him.

* * *

They hadn't marched on for more than a few miles when they saw the city of Jericho in the distance. Officials were watching for them from the high walls that surrounded the city.

Balthasar, Melchior, and Gaspar separated the caravan into three smaller groups. They decided to proceed in smaller groups and hoped to reduce the attention that they were attracting.

Balthasar attempted to pass by the city first. There was an Eastern gate and a Western gate. He did not want to pass through the city, but took the road that wound around the city next to the walls. When they did not enter the gates, a Roman soldier ran off to report it.

Melchior saw what happened and held back until

Balthasar was around the curve of the city. He approached and stopped at the Eastern Gate.

A Roman Legionnaire stepped forward to greet him.

"Shall I announce your presence to the representative of Herod for Jericho?" the soldier asked.

"No thank you," said Melchior.

They marched around to the other side and saw that Balthasar was stopped by a Centurion.

Balthasar looked back and saw Melchior and smiled. He turned his camel and headed into the city.

Gaspar caught up with Melchior.

"What is he doing?"

"I don't know. I thought for certain we were going to bypass the city, but they're moving in."

Finally, the two caught up to Balthasar. There was a great commotion at the gate. The entrance was filled with camels.

"I decided we should have lunch. Let's stop here for a while and refresh ourselves. The men haven't had a well-cooked meal in a long time."

"We are stopping because the men haven't had a good meal?"

Gaspar was incredulous.

"It's more than that. They say that there isn't a place to stay in all of Jerusalem. The crowds are huge and there is confusion about the land due to the Census Proclamation. I would like to enter Jerusalem in the early part of the day rather than late tonight."

"Why is that?" Gaspar asked.

"We can pack up, enter the city early and meet this Roman Governor, Herod the Great. We can present

ourselves to his court, get through with all the formalities, and leave at the end of the day when the star becomes more visible."

It seemed reasonable.

"Where will we make camp?" Melchior asked.

"Outside the city, on one of the hills."

They agreed with Balthasar's reasoning. Already the men had started to tether the animals. Jamil's yogurt pots were washed and fresh milk and a little yogurt culture were placed in them. The hot sun would cook the milk and by the next day, it would be fine yogurt.

The Roman Centurion suggested where they could eat. He discreetly tried to join them, but soon found out that the Magean Princes would not deign to dine with his rank.

"He did everything he could to find out what our business was," Melchior said with a laugh.

"I may be the oldest, but I have the tightest lips," Gaspar said with a sly smile.

"You gave him just enough to keep him wondering. You were teasing him," Balthasar said.

"Not really. He just asked poorly worded questions."

The old Magi was not trying to tease the Centurion. He wanted to let the young man know that he wasn't of high enough rank to speak with Gaspar about the purpose of the caravan. He had, however, shown the Roman that they were on a mission of peace, unarmed, and in no way meant to interfere with the political situation in Judea. In the process, Gaspar was able to understand a little more of the confusing politics of this turbulent region.

The caravan left the city for the brief trip over to Jerusalem. A short time later, they saw the shining city on a

hill, Jerusalem. They pitched their camp on the East side of the city in the small valley nestled on the side of the Mount of Olives.

*"Yet in thy dark streets shineth the everlasting Light;
The hopes and fears of all the years,
are met in thee tonight."*

11

The Little Town of Bethlehem

People from Jerusalem were scurrying to get to Bethlehem and other small towns. They were all doing the same thing . . . looking for a place to spend the night. The inns in Jerusalem were overflowing. The overflow had spread out into the countryside toward Caesarea and other towns. As the evening approached, the knowledge that it was first come, first serve drove people to rush along the road.

Joseph watched Mary for signs that they should stop. For the first two miles, she was fine. She smiled at him and tried to be supportive. She knew that men were more frightened of childbirth than women.

They were not even halfway there when Mary let out a little gasp. Joseph stopped the donkey and waited, not knowing what to do.

"That was a strong one," she said. There was relief in her voice and a comforting smile on her face that was put there just for Joseph. She rubbed her stomach and talked to Jesus.

They started on again. She did not have another one for about ten minutes. They were reduced to moving between contractions.

Mary was uncomfortable. She was rubbing her back when the contractions started. She got off the donkey and walked for a while. That seemed easier, but then a

contraction came and she had to stop. This went on for the next two hours. They were getting closer, but so was darkness.

Joseph offered her a shawl to cover her from the chill in the air.

"I'm fine. Let's keep going Joseph."

He saw that she was warm, sweating more than he had ever seen.

Other travelers on the road either did not notice or pretended not to. Darkness had suddenly descended like a heavy curtain. They were on the road alone. No one traveled after dark by choice. There were no giant candles like those used in the city of Rome. There was only the moon, the stars, and some lights in the windows of houses up ahead.

The couple passed a tall pillar. It was the tomb of Rachel. They were almost there. This was the last landmark outside the town.

Joseph stopped the donkey again and waited. They were coming closer now.

"Are you in pain?" he asked naively.

"I breathe in when they start and then softly sing the psalm while the contraction comes," she was smiling sweetly.

Joseph knew she was still trying to take care of her husband. It was simply her nature.

The entry into Bethlehem was uneventful. There was no wall or gate, just more houses and shops. The couple walked on toward the center of town. There was a small plaza or marketplace surrounded by small shops. The little town had three inns and a few eating establishments.

Joseph settled Mary down near an old well in the center of what could almost be called the town square. He placed their bedrolls and a pack next to her to support her back.

"Are you comfortable?"

"Yes."

She motioned for him to go find a room.

Joseph rushed over to the first inn. He opened the door and was faced with an innkeeper who simply shook his head.

"I need a room," Joseph said.

"We're full beyond capacity. Try the other two inns."

The door was closed abruptly.

Joseph turned on his heels and dashed out. He smiled at Mary and ran to the next inn. He found the door locked. He knocked.

A moment later, an old man with a big grin and a missing tooth opened the door.

He said, "Sorry, no room, but we are serving food and we have the best wine in town."

Joseph hurried off to the last place. It looked like the most expensive of the three. He prayed they had a room. When he came to the door, he found it bolted for the night, but it had a cord that ran inside for a visitor's bell. He pulled the cord to alert the innkeeper. He waited for a brief moment and pulled the cord again. He heard the bell ring softly within.

"For the love of God, a little patience," the voice said on the other side.

"I desperately need a room," Joseph said.

"You and half the Roman empire. We're full," the voice said.

The door didn't even open. Frustrated, he knocked loudly.

A small wooden window slid open, and a pair of large brown eyes looked out at Joseph.

"What part of 'we're full' didn't you understand?" the voice said. This time Joseph realized that the voice was young, and belonged to a boy who stared at him. His name was Joab.

"I have a wife and she is with child," Joseph pleaded.

A blank expression faced him. He had no idea what it implied.

"I need to speak with the proprietor, boy. Go get him."

Joseph raised his walking stick to knock even louder on the door. This shook the boy up. He ran to find the owner.

"Was my boy impolite?" the owner asked when he opened the door. He did not let Joseph in but rather stepped outside to see what was going on.

"We need a room."

"We are filled. I've even rented out my personal space. Don't you have family? Most travelers are staying with their families."

Joseph could see he wasn't getting anywhere.

"My wife is expecting our child, soon," said Joseph.

Mary looked comfortable and smiled at the man. She didn't look like she was going to deliver any minute. She had a contraction and started breathing to control the pain and the innkeeper understood.

He opened the door wide and beckoned Joseph in. "Sir, look into the courtyard. There are people bedding down for the night in the central courtyard. All the rooms are full and they are sleeping in the open courtyard."

"We have no room for you . . . to deliver a baby, you need privacy and peace and quiet."

When they went back outside, the donkey brayed loudly. It caught the innkeeper's attention.

"I have a stable for your beast. The straw is soft, and it is warm. You would be safe and away from prying eyes until someone leaves and a room becomes available."

Mary was having another contraction. She nodded to him that it was okay. Anything would do.

"I'll get my boy, Joab, to show you the way. Do you need any food or blankets?"

They were grateful for any help.

Joab came out to show them where the stable was. He had the habit of talking incessantly, but when he saw Mary's condition, he kept quiet.

"I'll take the donkey. The stables are just around the back at the end of the field," Joab said. He motioned for them to take the street next to the inn.

Joseph got Mary and rounded the corner to follow him.

Behind the inn was a small field used for grazing and perhaps a vegetable garden in the spring. The hills of Bethlehem jutted out further back and recessed within were small caves. Each of the caves had a small fence set up to keep the animals in. The caves provided shelter from the elements for the animals.

Further along, the street opened to the vast fields of Bethlehem that rose into the mountains. They were used to graze sheep and were barren compared to the fields below the town where the orchard and vineyards were.

Joab looked at the stables. He felt guilty that he was bringing the couple to such squalid conditions.

"My friends and I would sometimes sleep out under the stars. If the weather turned bad, we would run to the stables. Do not worry, it will be warm." His good heart tried to comfort them.

"I'm sure it will be just perfect," Mary said.

She thought for a moment about God's ways. She was thinking about the prophet Elijah. Humble beginnings. God is heard in the whisper, not in the tempest.

When they got closer, Joseph realized that what looked like three caves was one large grotto that had been subdivided into three. One part was empty, one had some sheep and one had an ox that the innkeeper kept. Joab led them to the empty cave in the middle.

"If it gets cold, you can bring the sheep in and let them sleep near you. If you can coax the ox to lie closer to the gate, the place will warm up."

Joseph thanked him for his advice. He was a carpenter, not an ox-driver. The ox could sleep where it wanted.

Mary motioned for Joseph to help her lie down on the straw. She settled down near the back of the small grotto. There was plenty of clean straw. She thanked Joab, who ran off to the inn.

"Hold my hands, Joseph," she said.

"The pains are coming closer?" he asked.

"A little. I think it will be a long night, so there is no use worrying now."

Mary let his hands go and relaxed. This would happen many times over the next few hours.

Joseph unburdened the donkey and set things up the best he could. The donkey was tethered near the front

and would hopefully provide some protection from the elements.

He looked around the stable to see what else was there. He found a chest with sheers for the sheep. There was another box filled with swaddling cloth. Mothers used the swaddling cloth to wrap their babies' limbs to make their arms grow straight. The cloth found in the sheep's stable was used to wrap newborn sheep to keep their limbs from moving before they were brought to the temple for sacrifice. Joseph held the cloth up and showed it to Mary.

"We can keep the baby warm in those," Mary said.

The infant would start his life wrapped with the swaddling cloth of a sacrificial lamb.

Joseph held up a small manger where the baby lambs were kept warm while they were being examined.

"We can use that as a crib. Put some fresh straw in it and bring it over next to me."

Mary's labor progressed until shortly after midnight, when its intensity increased. She had entered transition. The contractions were coming much closer now. Joseph felt helpless to do anything, other than comfort his wife and pray.

Every mother and every baby born went through this, he rationalized. He was still just as nervous as any soon-to-be father. He prayed with each contraction, trying to stay calm. He was amazed at how serene Mary was despite the intensity of childbirth. This young, first-time mother was caring for him, letting him know that she would be all right.

He looked around at the stable and suddenly felt a deep spiritual comfort. He saw the stable as a small piece

of paradise. He heard Mary's tone change. She was pushing. He wanted to jump up and do something, anything. She took his hands and squeezed them tightly. *My God, the baby is almost here!*

Suddenly, the sound of the blessed mother's straining was overwhelmed by the sound of angels singing . . . the sweet cry of a newborn . . . and the soft tears of joy of a mother taking her baby into her arms for the very first time.

A flash of what looked like lightning lit up the clear December sky. Shepherds who were tending their flocks in the adjacent fields were startled. There was another flash, softer, but it lasted much longer.

"What is this?" asked an old shepherd. He was looking up at the sky.

The men who had been sleeping woke up to watch the lights. They waited for thunder and when none came, they were confused and afraid. The illumination increased. Their small camp was engulfed in soft light. It intensified.

Suddenly, an angel appeared above them. Their terror was so great they could not run. They were paralyzed by their fear, forced to listen.

"Be not afraid. I bring you tidings of great joy. I bring you news of joy to all the world. Today in the town of David, a Savior has been born to you. He is Christ the Lord."

The men huddled together, overwhelmed by what they saw.

"This will be a sign to you men. You will find a baby wrapped in swaddling clothes and lying in a manger."

Suddenly, a great company of heavenly hosts appeared all around the angel. They filled the sky with singing that sounded like bells, harps, and celestial voices.

The men heard the voices loudly proclaim, "Glory to God in the highest, and on earth, peace to men of good will."

When the angels left them and went back into heaven, the shepherds jumped up and looked at each other, dumbfounded.

Finally, one of them said, "The town of David is our Bethlehem."

"Let's go to Bethlehem and see this birth that the Lord has told us about."

The shepherds hurried off down the side of the hills and found the stables where Mary, Joseph, and the newborn baby Jesus were. Baby Jesus was lying in the manger sleeping peacefully. Joseph was tending to his wife, doing the best that he could.

The oldest of the shepherds, named Benjamin, knocked softly on the makeshift gate. Joseph worried that perhaps the stable and manger belonged to this shepherd.

"Please, sir, my wife has just given birth and we are using the manger for a crib," Joseph said.

"Glory to God. This is the one," shepherd Benjamin said to the others.

He explained to Joseph and Mary what they had seen in the hills and begged them to please see the Christ child.

"Let them in Joseph. Make sure that you are quiet, men. The baby is sleeping," said Mary.

In her heart, she knew that the prophecy had been fulfilled. Today, the Messiah was born in Bethlehem.

Matthew 2:1
*"When Jesus was born in Bethlehem of Judea,
in the days of King Herod, behold,
Magi from the East arrived in Jerusalem."*

12
ENTERING JERUSALEM

The caravan arrived at Jerusalem, the City of Seven Gates. Word spread quickly that the caravan was going to camp outside the northern gate. Even though the Magi were unannounced, they created a stir throughout the city. Jerusalem was a center of political importance to Jews worldwide. What was the political purpose of this caravan of Eastern Magi? Speculation about the nature of the caravan was widespread among the local politicians. Advisers to Herod scrambled to learn the purpose of an unexpected visit by royalty.

The next morning, the caravan entered the city and was met by officials of the Roman Empire. Stating their authority as representatives of Herod the Great, the officials politely demanded an explanation for the Magi's entrance into their region. They made it seem as though they had come to extend hospitality to the Oriental dignitaries, but their goal was to understand the intent of this visit. They already knew that the Magi came without armed forces or bodyguards. Even a peaceful visit, though, could cause Herod to pay a political price. Herod did not like to pay. He preferred to extract payment from others.

The representatives of the Roman Governor were impressed with the visitor's wealth. They recognized that the travelers had vast economic resources and should be accorded the utmost respect. Since Roman hospitality

was given based on one's station in life, they were very gracious. The Governor would not embarrass his emperor with poor treatment of dignitaries.

Gaspar and Melchior did most of the talking. Balthasar remained polite, but aloof, as he watched the exchange. They were invited to the residence of Herod at the Hasmoneam Palace. The emissaries of the Governor correctly understood the royal status of their guests and acted appropriately, inviting all twelve Magi to dine with the Governor.

The huge caravan paraded through the city, entering at the gate next to the Fortress of Antonia. The Roman legions, with their red banners unfurled against the blue sky, provided a stark military contrast to the brilliant colors of the Magi. The vestments worn by the Magi were so luxurious that merchants and shoppers alike stopped their activities and stared at the travelers parading by.

Jamil could scarcely believe his eyes. This was indeed a magnificent city. He had listened to Abdul and Nemir speak about it, but he had no idea how wonderful it was until they entered the gates.

Jamil felt strange walking on the Roman roads. His hooves were used to the desert sand and dirt roads. He had never been on any ground that was covered by stone. Here in the city, the stone was stranger still. It was worn smooth.

Man-made coverings for the earth; how strange.

"Little one, are you well?" asked Heba.

"I feel confused by this place, Heba, though I don't know why," said Jamil.

"It is a confounding place, Jamil," said Heba. "It is

difficult for a camel to adapt to an environment like this. We are not suited to live in cities; we are suited for the desert. The Sustainer gave us enormous resources for the right kind of environment. This is not one of them."

"Why are there so many horses and so few camels?" asked Jamil. "Don't the men here need camels to carry their burdens?"

"Every place is different, my little friend. Each corner of God's world is blessed with different forms of life, all working together to carry out the will of the Divine. All places have different needs. In our travels, we pass through places where the horse is far more useful than the camel. Other places have cattle and oxen carrying the burden for man."

"There are horses and people everywhere. It doesn't feel right at all," said the little camel.

Jamil couldn't help staring at all the people. They were staring at him, too.

At the same time, the caravan drew considerable attention from the people of Jerusalem. The spectators realized that the kings were from India, Persia, and Arabia. It was obvious that the Magi were not on a trade mission, because they were not carrying costly items to be used as assets for barter. The twelve princes were traveling with one extra camel and a servant or driver for each; hardly the entourage of a merchant caravan or commercial enterprise.

The city was buzzing with activity. There were merchants everywhere. The caravan slowed as it entered more congested areas. They passed the Temple of Solomon, a magnificent edifice originally constructed to contain the

Ark of Covenant. Outside the Temple, following Jewish tradition, vendors sold live animals for sacrifice at the altar. Since Roman currency carried the figure of Caesar, considered a god, Jews could not use it in the temple. Money changers exchanged money so that people could buy the animal of their choice without violating the Law of God.

This neighborhood was a hub of activity. There was constant commotion. The marketplace seemed alive, like a giant creature. The bakeries and inns added to the liveliness of the area with delightful fragrances and delicious aromas.

Gaspar called Melchior and Balthasar to join him as they slowly meandered through the great city.

"Sirs, we must not give the name of the newborn King. Rather, I think it wise if we simply tell of his birth and how our tradition had prophesied it for many years," Gaspar advised his friends.

Balthasar nodded in agreement with the oldest wise man. "This is an extraordinary land known for its intrigue and therefore discretion would be best. It would be wise to speak only in generalities."

"Maybe you speak too quickly," said Melchior. "We should wait to see the intentions of the Roman magistrate before we decide what to do."

"This is a land ruled by power, as you can see from the Roman legion," said Gaspar. "We should be very careful. This is the only land we have traveled through where there were so many soldiers. Caesar's renown as a conquering ruler stands on its own."

"He is also worshipped as a god by his people," said Melchior.

"The Roman citizens consider him divine. With that kind of power, who knows what type this Herod will turn out to be," said Gaspar.

"Yes, and Herod had himself referred to as 'the great'," said Melchior with a laugh.

"We approach the palace, sirs. Please inform the other Magi to be cautious and discreet."

* * *

Jamil started to act up. It was Abdul's task to quiet him down. When the party stopped in front of the outer gate to the Hasmoneam Palace, the Roman soldiers examined the camels. When they got to Jamil, they looked closely. They were curious about the contraption. Jamil did not appreciate the attention. He was skittish. Heba was tethered to him, and Nemir and Abdul made both animals kneel and then lie down. Kneeling usually calmed a camel down.

"I should have spit at him, right Heba?" asked Jamil.

"Not a good idea."

"It seemed like a good idea to me. Why are we stopped?"

"We have arrived at the palace where the Magi will dine."

"This is not like any oasis I've ever seen. There are so many people. I feel like the center of attention. I am not sure I deserve it, nor do I want it."

Jamil's thoughts were racing again.

"You wanted to be a racer when you grew up. This is the kind of attention you'd get."

"I can handle it. I'm just a little worried about what these people will do."

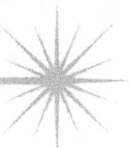

"Just be still. Nemir has never let any harm come your way," said Heba.

Jamil gave Heba a doubtful look.

"The people are admiring the yogurt carrier. It is so finely crafted. The soldiers are appraising the fabric, the construction of the frame, and the design of the device."

"Do you think the Magi will tell them that they were instructed to build it, and each was given a part to play in the procuring of the fabric?"

"Of course not."

"How do you know that?" asked Jamil.

"I listen to the discussions while you sleep or fret," said Heba.

"You're right. I don't bother with that stuff," said Jamil. "I worry about the next river, or what may happen on our way back."

"You need to spend more time here in the present instead of in the future, dreaming about what might happen," said Heba.

"But I can't help wondering about the rest of the trip."

"You need not wonder about the rest of the trip," said Heba. "You need to stay focused on what you do from moment to moment."

"Are you going to start that stuff about living one day at a time, and not projecting, and one step . . . "

"Slow down. The Sustainer will bring you all the peace and serenity you need if you allow it."

Jamil did not get a lecture this time because Heba sensed that something had changed. It had happened when he walked out of the Jordan River. He was a new camel. He was reborn into a world of greater faith and trust.

"How do you do it?" Jamil asked.

"Do what?" she asked.

"Stay so calm."

"I used to worry about tomorrow. Then I decided to trust that the Sustainer would guide me in the direction of his will." Heba paused. "And life got easier."

"It already is getting easier. Except that I am wearing this strange device."

"Fear, no matter how grounded in reality, is your mind's way of robbing you of the serenity you deserve."

"I'd like to be serene, but you've got to admit I may be right about this contraption."

"Being right is not nearly as important as being happy. Your mind focuses on fear to distract you, to prove that you have a right to be unhappy. You need to ask what is the solution to this fear of being harmed."

"I have no solution," said Jamil. "All I know is that I have to lie still while throngs of people try to touch me and this thing."

He paused and looked away. He was somewhere else in his mind.

"What is it that you think might make you feel better, make you happy?"

"I'd like to go back to the river," he said. "I know that sounds stupid. But right about now, I'd love nothing more than to immerse myself in a pool of crystal-clear water. I don't even know why I crave it."

"You crave it because you are a camel, and we crave water. The explanation doesn't need to be any deeper than that," replied Heba.

"I guess I always craved it."

"As soon as you feel afraid, nervous, bored, or anything that doesn't seem right, you find yourself craving water. I used to tell myself 'Just a little,'" said Heba. "And then I would lose control. I tried to drink as much as I could. It was always a little more and never enough. I would fight to stay at the water trough, so out of control that I was almost sold off to be slaughtered. I created havoc wherever I went."

"I thought you were a racing camel."

"Pretty bad isn't it if a racing camel gets sold off to slaughter?"

"I can't believe that you were ever that bad."

"I wasn't bad. My behavior was. It was a matter of not being willing to admit that I was born a camel. I needed to be realistic and honest. As soon as I did, life started to work."

Heba looked at her young friend and continued. "If I had been in your situation, I would have rebelled. I was the kind of camel who found any excuse to lose control."

"What did you do, Heba?" asked Jamil.

"Well, I used anything as an excuse to spit," said Heba.

"I love to spit too."

It was true. It was part of a camel's nature to spit.

"I loved to feel my rage. I was angry all the time. I had an uncontrollable desire to jump up and start kicking people who annoyed me."

"Exactly. I'd like to jump up and go crazy. I'd like to let everyone know that they can't do whatever they like with me."

"Yes. Your mind is trying to rationalize how you would be justified in creating a disturbance."

"Exactly."

"You worry a lot too, Jamil."

"I do. It is as though I keep worrying, just to have something to be upset about. Did you do that?"

"I still have to watch it. I am a camel."

They both laughed.

"I thrive on being upset. There's no real reason," said Jamil.

"There isn't any reason, little one," said Heba. "If there were, then you would have a good excuse to run off to the river."

"Why is it that ever since we came into the city, I have had this urge to drink? I don't understand it. It has been upon me like a swarm of flies, annoying and everywhere at once."

Heba motioned first to the corner of the large open plaza where they were tethered, to a spot where women and children dipped buckets into a well. She motioned to some statues, which had water running out of various holes and around the base, and continued,

"When man builds cities, he builds them around sources of water. The cities may change. The rulers may change, but the water sources do not. Man has associated his civilization with the ease of being able to drink. Water is very distracting. It plays on your mind without you even knowing it."

"It is as though I have a sixth sense about where to find water," said Jamil.

"Camels do have an instinct about water. It serves them in the desert. It is there that the Sustainer's will for you becomes powerful. In the desert, you discover your greatness."

"So, what do I do for now?" asked Jamil.

"Be patient, for the city and all its temptations will pass."

"This too shall pass," said Jamil with a smile.

"I think you are starting to get it," said Heba.

* * *

While the twelve Magi were inside with Herod and his court, Nemir, Abdul, and the other camel drivers tended the animals. They cautioned the mothers to keep their children away from them. The ornate embroidery and fine silks attracted the attention of the women, who had their husbands inquire about them. The children were curious to know about the exotic places where this beautiful fabric was made. A few of the drivers were telling stories that painted pictures of strange lands. It was the stuff of great adventure.

Inside the palace, Herod was charming, yet he kept an air of authority. When the dinner was over and the entertainment proved tiresome, Herod put an abrupt end to the festivities. He could tell they were not interested in the dancers and the harpist.

"Gaspar, you and your party seem weary. Would you like to make my palace your resting place for tonight?" asked Herod.

"That is quite kind, King Herod, but we plan to continue," said Gaspar. "We do our best navigation by the evening stars."

"Why is that?" asked Herod.

"Have your court astrologers not noticed the strange new phenomenon that has appeared in the evening sky?"

"They have mentioned something about it to me, but I am a busy man. My duties are to administer Judea for Augustus Caesar."

Herod feigned ignorance.

"Then you have noticed it?" said Balthasar.

Herod nodded. He searched for the right Magi to address.

"Would any of you care to explain to the astrologers of the Roman court what the phenomenon is all about?"

With that, one of the court astrologers, a learned man named Lucraticus, cleared his throat. Herod turned and addressed him with sarcasm.

"I suppose that Lucraticus, official astrologer to the Roman court of Judea, would like to explain to these learned Magi what the phenomenon is all about."

As he spoke, the turtledoves that had perched on the windowsills fluttered away as if sensing the wrath of the ruler.

"I, or rather we, the official Roman astrologers, have tried to explain the phenomenon to King Herod. But our beloved king has deemed our explanations false because of a troubling dream he had."

Herod was not pleased that he had mentioned his dream.

Lucraticus went on. He knew he was out on a limb, but his pride threw precaution to the wind.

"We believe that the star heralds a new era of importance for the kingdom of Judea within the magnificent Roman Empire. We believe that this star is the first sign of great events to be bestowed upon Judea. The Roman Empire's crowning jewel will be the city of Jerusalem.

Herod will be a prelate without equal in the history of the Roman Empire."

The astrologer was pleased with himself and his efforts to convince Herod of his grandiose position in the great scheme of things. The real purpose of his little speech was to show that he could flatter Herod more than the Magi could.

Herod was annoyed even more. Before he spoke, he took a deep breath and held it for a second. He scanned the Magi, hoping to find something that only he knew he needed.

"True, I have had a dream that has troubled me," said Herod.

Melchior watched Herod closely. He was dealing with a dangerous man who he did not plan on flattering. He was a sophisticated dream interpreter and listened closely as Herod continued.

"I have dreamed that this strange new star over the skies of Judea has fallen to earth."

A murmur went up from the Magi. They watched Melchior's face for signs of emotion. Was he going to speak?

"As the star fell, I noticed that it was a star of David."

"Referring to the kingdom of Judea," interrupted Lucraticus.

Herod clenched his jaws and glared at the Roman astrologer.

"As it fell, the points of the star gently turned upward. It glowed brilliantly as it slowly descended from the heavens. It fluttered to the ground and changed shape when it landed in Judea. It became a six-pronged crown with

twelve inset jewels of twelve different colors." Herod paused and looked at Melchior.

"There was more, wasn't there?" asked Melchior, who recognized that his youth annoyed Herod.

"Yes. I have not slept well since, and this was the part that confused me. The star was small and the emperor walked across the Mediterranean to step on it. No matter how much he stepped on the crown, it still glowed brilliantly. I realized I had tried to step on it first and it got brighter still."

"And so, you would like an interpretation of the dream?" said Melchior, being careful to show respect.

"I would reward you handsomely for an interpretation," said Herod to the young black Magus.

"That would be unnecessary," said Melchior. "Dreams are from the realm of the divinity. To be paid for an interpretation is blasphemy. This dream could be interpreted by any one of us with ease."

His words annoyed the court astrologers.

"Then please tell me. Of what strange events does this dream portend for me and the kingdom of Judea?" asked Herod.

"To place the dream in perspective, you must understand the purpose of our visit," said Melchior.

He looked to Gaspar to see if it was wise to continue. He received a nod.

"We have followed that celestial body for months now, believing it to be the fulfillment of the ancient prophecy of Hystapes. A king has been born to the Jews. Since the time of Noah and the great flood, these people have

awaited the descent of this leader from heaven. We are now in search of this child."

"You use the word search, but you must know the location if you have traveled so far to visit," said Herod carefully.

"We only know his approximate location."

"When you find him, I would like to send some emissaries to pay our respects. It would be customary for me to treat this individual with great respect, especially if he is to rise to the stature of their David or King Solomon."

By now, Melchior had become wary of the Roman magistrate, but he remained polite and dignified. He did not realize that Herod "the Great" already saw himself as the ruler who had risen to the stature of Solomon. That is why he expanded the Second Temple and built the Antonia Fortress.

"Would you like the interpretation of the rest of the dream?" Melchior asked.

"It is now clear that the star was the Star of David and that these people are fiercely protective of their religious beliefs. I do not think Caesar would try to suppress them in any way. The dream implies that he will let them be. I dare say though," said Herod hastily, "That this child must be honored because it is our policy to treat all dignitaries with the utmost respect."

There was a moment of silence in the room before Gaspar spoke.

"We do not know the exact location of the child at this time."

"We do believe that we are headed toward the vicinity of Bethlehem," said Balthasar, "But how we shall find him, once we are there, is not yet known to us."

"Well, then," said Herod, "I will provide you with an escort of Roman Auxilia or cavalry from my court. They will accompany you to Bethlehem. It is not an opportune time for the Roman Empire to pay formal homage because of the census."

"But we do not have his location," said Gaspar.

He was deliberately withholding the name Yeshua from the conversation for fear of Herod's intentions.

"That is quite all right," replied Herod. "On your way back again, be my guests and return to taste my hospitality. You can tell me his location then. In the meantime, my entire staff is overburdened by the census. I'm sorry, but it is not the best time for us to honor the child."

The Roman magistrate glanced at his astrologer and nodded almost imperceptibly. Herod rose, as did all the others.

"I take leave of you, gentlemen. My palace is open to you. If you change your mind and decide to stay the night to refresh yourselves, please do."

In another chamber, King Herod called together the chief priests and some teachers of the law.

"Where will the Jewish Messiah be born?" he demanded.

They told him that the prophet had written it would happen in Bethlehem of Judea.

He nodded that he was satisfied.

Outside, the camel drivers were waiting. The camels had been tended to, and the caravan was ready to leave. When the four Roman Auxilia joined the Magi, even more of a stir was created. They were mounted on magnificent steeds and wore Corinthian helmets, bronze chest plates, and bronze greaves to protect their legs. They carried a long

sword called a spatha. The only thing missing was their short spears. Rumor flew through the city that the Magi were going to visit a newborn baby who would one day rise to be the shining star of the Jewish people. The speculation rivaled the awe created by the caravan. Jerusalem was in turmoil that evening.

Jamil was brought to his knees and then to his feet by Nemir.

"Away, little one. Let us go. We will make a pretty sight for all these people to see. Let them wonder at your strange burden and all your fine silk. Let them wonder indeed."

Nemir enjoyed being the center of attention. He appreciated the eyes of the crowd on them both. So, he paraded Jamil around the other camels, urging them into line, showing off.

The twelve Magi came out in groups of four, as did the Roman Auxilia, who were their guides. They started marching south through the city. It was only six miles to the little town of Bethlehem.

Matthew 2:9
"After their audience with the king they set out.
And behold, the star that they had seen at its rising
preceded them, until it came and stopped over the place
where the child was."

13

THE CARAVAN ARRIVES IN BETHLEHEM

It was a warm dry evening as the caravan, joined by the Roman Auxilia on their beautiful mounts, slowly moved south. The hillsides were speckled with sheep. An occasional shepherd watched as the caravan moved down the stone road, which was not a major Roman thoroughfare. It still had the typical large blocks of granite embedded in it. The blocks were leveled off, as was the Roman custom. It made for easy travel, especially in a chariot.

The terrain from Jerusalem to Bethlehem was an open area with a few homes clustered together. These were inhabited by humble people who had etched out a hard living from Israel for centuries. The hills were fertile though, and the fruit trees, vineyards, and olive groves bore an abundance at harvest. God had blessed this little corner of the world. He now was blessing it far more profoundly.

The caravan proceeded in an orderly fashion. The contrast between the camels and the Roman horses was striking. The camels were almost comical, except for the fact that the riders were so dignified. The Magi riding them were almost three feet higher than the horsemen. The splendor of their robes made an unmistakably royal impression.

Gaspar spoke politely to the Roman cavalryman, while Balthasar spoke to the Magi, who had been traveling with

him. Arbakchest, the oldest, listened intently and looked as though he could tolerate no more.

"I have held my tongue, sir," he said, "But I do not believe that King Herod was pleased with the birth of this child."

"I, too, sensed this," said Balthasar, "And yet, when a man of his stature gives his word, it is the law."

"Are we so naïve as to believe that Herod gave his word to honor the child?" asked Akreho, who was known as a master of logic.

"My friend, we are not so naïve. Yet Herod did say it was his responsibility to extend the formal courtesies of the emperor to anyone of this child's stature."

Arbakchest again spoke.

"It is wise that we speak in our native tongue. I feel that the Romans are not committed to spiritual quests, but to material conquests. Herod may be the Jewish ruler but at heart, he is the magistrate for the Romans. They have not paid attention to this celestial phenomenon, though Herod has been distressed by his dream."

"The Romans have been busy with their census and have not had time to investigate the birth of the divine one," said Akreho.

"As a Jew, he should have been thrilled that this prophecy was coming to pass," said Astonkakodon.

"Do you believe that they have not heard of the child yet?" asked Balthasar.

"Perhaps they have," said Astonkakodon, the physician among the Magi. He had been listening with his head bent forward.

"Perchance someone from the village of Bethlehem has had contact with the child and realized his importance."

LAST GIFT OF THE MAGI   151

"I have thought about that. Anyone who has come in contact with the child would have been selected by the Almighty to participate in the child's destiny. I do not believe that the child would be subject to intrusions or harm by those who respect only worldly power."

"Balthasar, you are an idealist to the end," said Arbakchest. "We don't know if it is the child's fate to suffer during his lifetime."

"True, my friend. We cannot pretend to know God's mysteries. To assume that all will be easy is to assume that the forces of evil do not exist," said Balthasar. "Let us use caution."

Balthasar called to Melchior, who was having a quiet discussion of his own with Sadlak, Aksherosh, and Merodak. He moved his camel and they slowly came together. It was a strange sight, first, the heads of the camels moved together, followed by their bodies.

"What has your group been discussing?" said Balthasar

"We have been pondering the Roman magistrate's intentions, "said Melchior. "I do not trust the man."

Balthasar was pensive for a long moment.

"It might be wise to camp out for the night. We could thank the Romans in the morning and see if we could get them to leave."

Gaspar heard them and moved closer.

"Let me remind you, gentlemen, that I have given my word that when we pass through Jerusalem again, we will tell Herod of the location of the Child."

They were uneasy. They needed to focus their minds on the Messiach command and the ritual that they would soon perform.

Unknown to the Magi, the Roman Auxilia had been instructed to accompany them only as far as the town where the divine child lived. They had been ordered to turn back as soon as the general location was verified.

An Auxilia rode on horseback alongside Jamil, who became fidgety as the Roman examined his harness. He tried to butt the head of the horse, but the animal was quicker.

"This harness is making me the center of attention," said Jamil. "Will their curiosity never end?"

"Don't you think that maybe they have a right to be a little curious about the contraption?" said Heba.

"Well, probably."

He moved to spit at the horse, but it pulled back a bit.

"Jamil, he is a horse. He's got quick reflexes. You are wasting energy on things you have no control over."

"Don't I have the right to complain?" asked Jamil. *Here comes another annoying sermon.*

"You are right. But I'm not addressing the problem of right or wrong. I'm trying to get you to see the more basic problem of being happy or miserable."

Jamil liked being right so the little sermon wasn't so annoying.

"I'm right. I'm glad you realize that. So, stay with me on this idea Heba. I am being singled out by these Roman cavalrymen. And I don't have to like that, do I?"

Jamil had a smug look on his face.

"You don't have to like it, and that is my point. You can choose to be happy or miserable. But you don't have the faintest idea that you control how you respond to the situation," said Heba. "Here we are in Bethlehem. The journey

is almost complete and instead of being joyful, you are annoyed that people are looking at you."

Jamil started to speak, but the older camel swung his neck over, as a sign to keep quiet.

"This is a special caravan. You have been selected to carry this thing. Be grateful. Feel joy. You have a special task, no matter how insignificant it appears," said Heba. "That is the only response that makes sense. Trying to control the responses of others makes no sense at all."

"I don't think you understand me too well," said Jamil. "I am just trying to stay calm and relaxed. They have taught me to walk at this easy cadence, and I can't concentrate on what I am doing with this mounted soldier with all his shiny brass staring at me and what I am carrying. And now he is leaning over to pull on it."

"I see," said Heba. "You are just trying to stay calm and relaxed, and they are interfering with your ability to do so."

"Yes, that's right. I am trying to do my job without interference from others," said Jamil.

He spits at the horse and got him this time.

The horse tried to bite him. The Roman backed off.

"I hope he punishes his horse for lack of discipline."

"Blaming others is part of the problem here," said Heba. "It comes down to being wise enough to focus on what you can change and letting the rest be."

"Why is it that whenever I start to complain, you always correct me?" asked Jamil.

"I'm trying to help you use what you have learned in the desert in all your affairs. When truth learned by adversity

is carried into other areas of our lives, the Sustainer brings tremendous blessings and fantastic possibilities."

She paused for a moment to let this idea sink in.

"One must never take the great lessons in life as truths just for the moment. Truth transcends time. When a principle is universal, you can use it in other realms of your life."

"So, what is the universal value here that God is trying to get me to use?" asked Jamil.

He was curious to hear the older camel out because he sensed that life might be made easier.

"The principle simply stated is this: Be serene and accept the things you cannot control. Be courageous and change the things you can. Still your mind so that the Sustainer of life can give you the wisdom to know the difference between the two."

The caravan had grown still as they paused on the outskirts of the little town of Bethlehem.

Matthew 2:11
"... and on entering they saw the child with Mary his mother. They prostrated themselves and did him homage. Then they opened their treasures and offered him gifts of gold, frankincense, and myrrh.

14

THE MESSIACH COMMAND

Bethlehem was humble in every sense of the word. It was not a major city, but a simple village much like most of the small towns in Judea. Usually, the roadside leading to Bethlehem was quiet, though today there was more activity because of the census. The town had a tiny square that was the center of commerce and activity. Most of the citizenry were shepherds or farmers. Many families were sharing their modest homes with relatives who had traveled great distances. There was no wall, only a large gate announcing the entrance to the town. There were not even Roman soldiers garrisoned there.

One of the Roman cavalrymen lifted his hand to signal a halt. The caravan stopped. The leader of the Auxilia, a man named Camius, turned his horse sideways and spoke to the Magi.

"Gentlemen, as instructed by Herod the Great, we have conducted you safely to this town. Since we have no further business here, we will take leave of you."

A soft murmur went through the caravan. The Magi looked at each other in disbelief. They had not expected the caravan to be released by the Romans.

The Roman nodded to another cavalryman who asked, "What are you doing with this device?"

It was the long-awaited question. The device was the

obvious item that everyone pretended did not exist or matter. Why did they wait so long to ask?

"We are carrying yogurt. It is a very important part of our diet too," said Gaspar. "Would you care to sample it?"

The cavalryman looked at Camius, who nodded for him to taste it. He reached into the pot with his knife. With a smile and a tilt of the head, he agreed that it was indeed quite good.

"And this other side, what do you carry here?"

When the Roman Auxilia looked inside, he found a small package. It had been purchased by Nemir while the Magi met with Herod.

Gaspar looked around to see who was responsible for putting items in the holder.

"Sir, I thought it would be a fine treat for the men to break bread and drink a cup of wine," said Nemir.

"So, this side is a bread and wine holder. Rather elegant," said the Auxilia. He suppressed his skepticism.

The men were quiet for a moment.

Camius spoke again. "You are respectfully invited to partake of King Herod's hospitality on your return. Please honor us with your presence at the Roman magistrate's palace, the Hasmoneam, when you pass through Jerusalem. At that time, we will restock you with provisions for your journey as an expression of the emperor's hospitality. We would want the bread and wine you carry back to the east to be the finest in Caesar's empire." There was a sardonic look on his face.

The four horses joined in a side-by-side formation and marched off at a slow canter.

The Magi sat on their camels and surveyed the town. On

the outskirts, there were a few houses clustered together. From their vantage point, they could see a large pillar standing alongside the road leading into the village.

Melchior stopped a traveler, who was walking along the road. He asked, "What is that pillar, sir?"

"It marks the tomb of Rachel,' he said. Then realizing that these strangers did not know the local history, he added, "She was an important ancestor in the House of David that ruled here."

'So where should we look for this child," asked Gaspar.

Balthasar lifted himself and looked over Gaspar's shoulder. "The town has a piazza, maybe we should start there before it gets too dark."

As they moved along the road to the piazza or town square, the sun slowly set over the hills in the west. The sky began to glow crimson, heralding the celebration of another day's end. However, for the Magi, this day was long from over. A solemnity had come over them. It was mixed with a mounting joy.

The star, which always seemed to be moving, appeared to be stationary near the back of the town of Bethlehem.

The departure of the Roman Cavalry left the Magi free to talk openly about the ritual of the Messiach Command. For centuries, they had practiced the ceremony on the twenty-third of July on the Mountain of Victories. Everyone knew that this evening would be the most special night of their lives. What had been ritual before would be a reality this evening. What had been the careful protection of an ancient tradition handed down from the time of Noah would be a present-day celebration of joy and gratitude. They were excited about finding the newborn

babe. They were grateful that the Creator had kept his word to fulfill the promise of divine intercession for the world.

The Magi were bringing twelve gifts to the newborn Jewish Messiah. These twelve gifts had been identified centuries ago for the child. His birth had been anxiously awaited by more than just the Jewish people. This child belonged to all humanity. The Magi represented all the races of man in the known world and therefore, all of humanity.

Gaspar, Melchior, and Balthasar consulted with each other. They decided to approach an elderly lady.

"Woman, we are looking for a newborn boy who is the heir to the throne of David," asked Gaspar.

She shook her head at them in disbelief. "There has been no king from David's House for quite some time. We are under Roman occupation."

"Still, we need to find a baby who was born recently," said Gaspar who realized that their search might indeed prove frustrating.

"And what do you strangers mean to do when you find this boy?" asked the woman. She was suspicious of strangers.

"We mean him no harm, good woman," said Melchior. "We have brought him some gifts and some items that are his by birthright."

"Well, if you have some of his belongings, then you should know his family and who he is. What is the child's name, sir?" she asked.

Some other people gathered to listen. Among them was the young boy, Joab, who worked at the inn. Seeing the

strangers as an opportunity for his employer to gain revenue, he approached the crowd.

"What is it these men need, a place to stay?" he said raising his voice just a bit.

"No, they want to find a newborn king. They say they have brought him some gifts," said the old woman.

She was still eyeing the Magi suspiciously and was not getting too close to the camels.

"No new kings born here," said Joab, "But if you gentlemen would like a warm meal and a room, I can bring you to the inn. We are full, but I might be able to get my master to extend his hospitality."

The boy was already wondering who they would throw out to accommodate these wealthy travelers.

"My master is well informed. He knows everyone in town and will know who recently bore a child."

"It can't hurt to speak with the man," said Gaspar.

He was looking up at the sky, hoping the star would guide them to the exact house, now that it had stopped moving.

"Lead on boy," said Melchior. "We can all use a good meal." He was smiling at the lad's industrious spirit.

As the caravan entered the square, more people gathered around to see them. The young boy brought his master out to meet the Magi. They were descending from their desert mounts, looking at the inn.

"Sirs, I apologize for the boy here. We haven't had rooms at our inn for days. There is a census going on and everyone and his cousin have returned to Bethlehem."

"Could you indicate where we can have our camels stabled? We would prefer an open field. They will need some water and feed so that the men can attend to them."

"I can get you supplies of feed. Would you gentlemen be staying for dinner?" asked the innkeeper.

"Yes," said Gaspar. "We can camp just outside of town if you can show us a place to stable the camels."

"Yes, no problem. Please come in."

The innkeeper noted the elaborate silks and was rejoicing at his good fortune to prepare a meal for these men.

"Before we eat, we must find a newborn baby," said Melchior as they entered the inn.

"What do you need a newborn for?" he asked with concern.

"We bring him gifts."

"Who are the parents?" the innkeeper said.

"We do not know their names."

"In the morning, you can talk to the census officials and find out who has had babies. They will know. They know everyone."

He was trying to stall them until he could find out what they really wanted.

Joab came over to the innkeeper and whispered to him.

"We have a problem with lodging the animals, sir. Remember that couple."

"Just ask them to leave. They must have family somewhere in town. These men need the stable."

The boy whispered again into his master's ear. The innkeeper's wife walked over and pulled Joab away.

"You can not ask them to leave. I told them that they could stay as long as she needed. The poor girl just had her baby. She must stay where she is. She needs to rest."

The innkeeper knew not to argue with his wife over these matters.

"Sirs, we have a problem with the stable for your animals. It seems that it is still occupied by this poor couple who were searching for a place to stay. We had no rooms, so I thought that they could bed down in the stable. I felt sorry for them because she was in the family way, if you know what I mean. The straw was clean, and I figured that they could keep warm there."

"Yes, but can't you find them a better place so we can take care of the animals?" asked Balthasar.

"The woman had her child only yesterday. We allowed the little family to stay there. It was more private. They were not planning on moving on until the census was finished."

Joseph had just entered the back of the inn to purchase some bread. He walked over to see what was going on. He had heard them speak of a child and immediately became concerned.

The innkeeper's wife told him what was going on and assured him they could stay in the stable. Joseph approached cautiously. He was put off by the splendor of their robes and the sight of the camels outside. A simple man, he could not conceive of what they might want, but he approached anyway.

The innkeeper noticed Joseph standing there.

"This is the father of the newborn baby," said the innkeeper, motioning for Joseph to come over.

"Congratulations on the birth of your baby. Was it a boy or a girl?"

"A baby boy, sir," said Joseph. He smiled proudly.

The other Magi immediately paid close attention.

"May I ask, are you by any chance a descendent of the House of David?"

"Yes sir, I am, but just about everyone in town tonight is a descendant of David because of the census."

"I am Gaspar of India. This is Balthasar of Persia and Melchior of Sebain Arabia."

"My name is Joseph, of Nazareth."

"We were looking for a certain newborn," said Gaspar gently.

"There is probably more than one newborn in this village, sir," said Joseph.

"We are looking to pay our respects to the one called Yeshua, who was born under the new celestial body that shines overhead," said Gaspar.

"My son is named Jesus, which is a modern form of the Hebrew name Yehoshuah. Yeshua is an old nickname that was used for Yehoshuah," said Joseph.

He paused and looked at the assembly of men. The psalm came back to him: "May the kings of Tarshish and the islands bring tribute, the kings of Arabia and Seba offer gifts."

"But how could you have known his name? You are from faraway lands, and we are simple village people who earn a living by the sweat of our brows. We are not royalty."

"Was your little child Jesus born under this brilliant new star?"

"Yes. When he was born, it was the time of night when the star was directly overhead," said Joseph.

A murmur went through the small group that had gathered to watch.

"Will you take us to see him?" asked Gaspar.

Joseph hesitated for a moment.

Melchior stepped forward.

"Would you honor us by presenting our party to your child? We have journeyed many months to arrive at this destination, and we would like to pay tribute to him."

"You wish to pay tribute?"

Joseph was confused by the idea.

"Yes. We wish to show our respect," added Balthasar.

Joseph nodded. He was worried, but thought Mary would know what to do.

"The boy here will show you to the stable. I would like a few moments to see if my wife is able to receive any guests." Joseph went out to speak with Mary.

With that, the Magi and Joab left the inn and went out front to the men.

"Lead my men to where we can set up camp for the night. Then show us to this stable, young man," said Gaspar.

They were led to a side street and down the road a short distance. They saw the large open field off to the back, with the stable caves where Mary and Jesus were. To the side of these stables were open areas for grazing that suited their needs. The Magi decided to be discrete and wait for Joseph to let them know if they could approach.

Joseph went out the back and into the stable where Mary and baby Jesus were.

"Mary, there are these men are from far off in the East. They were looking for a newborn babe who had been born under that wonderful celestial body. They knew his name was Yeshua and that he was a descendant of the House of David. The innkeeper's wife pointed me out to them. They want to pay tribute to little Jesus and brought the baby some gifts."

Mary smiled. The kings of Arabia and Seba offer gifts.

Mary already knew the importance of the arrival of the Magi. This was just the first of many miraculous events in her child's life. She would have to learn to contend with the unusual and sometimes difficult situations that his destiny would bring. She was also the wife of Joseph and the woman of the house.

"You invite all these men here and we have no way to serve them or show them hospitality," she said softly, looking at their squalid surroundings. Somehow, she knew it was going to be all right.

While waiting for Joseph to reappear, each of the Magi went to his respective camel. There was a small commotion as they talked among themselves. The Magi retrieved special items from the loads that the camels were carrying. They formed three neat lines, with Gaspar, Melchior, and Balthasar at the head.

Joseph walked back out to meet the men.

They bowed solemnly and walked the rest of the distance to where the child was. It was a strange sight to behold: twelve regally robed Magi, with a large herd of camels being led by drivers. The Magi's dignity seemed out of place in the humble surroundings.

Before entering the stable, Joseph lifted his belongings onto his shoulder. He moved them out of the way so that all the Magi could enter. One of the Magi motioned for a servant to carry Joseph's load, but he would have none of it.

Joseph wondered what sort of strange fortune awaited him and his family. It was a man's duty to protect his household. Joseph did not feel endangered, just out of place. He felt that he should be leading them to a luxurious

palace of some sort, instead of to his small grotto on the edge of town. It was not a well-built dwelling with a carpenter's woodwork everywhere evident. It was a cave with gates and three stalls. It was certainly not fit for his wife and child. He wanted to bring Mary and his child home to Nazareth, where he had built a house for himself. But even that was small and humble. He wanted to give Mary a house that was cared for and well built; not a home that would never seem finished, as was the plight of many carpenters' homes. There was always a repair or modification to be done, and always something else he could envision doing.

The Magi waited patiently for him to move his things.

Joseph opened the gate to let the men in.

Mary wondered about the fulfillment of the prophecy in the psalm.

"The kings of Arabia and Seba offer gifts," she said softly to Jesus.

The contrast between the Jewish carpenter and the luxuriously appointed Magi was quite striking.

When Joseph saw Mary and the baby, he smiled. She questioned him with her eyes, then glanced over to the Magi and their entourage.

"You did not mention that there were so many," she said.

The group entered the stable and saw the child wrapped in swaddling cloth, asleep in a lamb's manger.

The camel drivers moved one of the camels towards the stable. It carried the large ornate backpack with two pots on the side. It was the only camel allowed close enough to see the blessed event.

Jamil turned back to Heba and the other camels and

described what he saw, "There is a beautiful baby boy, wrapped in swaddling cloth, being held by a young mother."

Joseph introduced his wife and child. "Sirs, this is my wife, Mary."

"And this is our son, Jesus," said Mary.

The Magi stood with their arms together in front of them. They bowed with utmost reverence. Each carried something wrapped in silk cloth. At Joseph's invitation, they slowly filed through past the gate and into the small area where the manger was. Their donkey moved away, and the ox backed up.

"Joseph just motioned for the Magi to rest, and they seated themselves on the floor," Jamil said.

Jesus was asleep. He stirred for a moment. Mary watched lovingly, vigilant lest he needed her attention. The men were quite comfortable.

"What are they doing now?" Heba asked.

"Gaspar is speaking."

Heba motioned for the other camels to settle down so they could hear.

"We are grateful to you for letting us visit. We are here to pay homage to this king," said Gaspar.

"You are our guests," said Joseph.

"We have come from India, Persia, and Arabia bearing special gifts that reflect the divine nature of your Child," said Melchior. "We have been traveling for a long time, following the new star. In our party, we have representatives of our religion, who are Magi or priests. Among us are our most illustrious astrologers, medical practitioners, and philosophers. Each has been specially chosen as a representative."

"Gaspar is explaining how they traveled such a long distance following the star," said Jamil.

Joseph and Mary listened patiently to the explanation. Jamil had to move out of the way so that the Magi could send the boy Joab back for some bread, fruit, and wine.

"They're going to eat some fruit," said Jamil. "It's making me hungry."

Young camels never tire of eating.

"Hey, now Melchior is going to explain the Messiach Command," Jamil whispered.

"Many years ago, the Oracle of Hystapes was traveling in a land north of here on his way to Tarsus. He was traversing a mountain pass during July. The sun had melted the snow from the high peaks of Ararat. This man spotted what he thought was a huge house on the side of the mountain. A terrible storm struck and left him stranded for a full day high above the slopes and above the mountain pass he had planned to take. The storm unsettled some land, and a small avalanche rocked the area where he sought protection. Part of the wooden house above had been destroyed by the avalanche and had fallen to the base of the slope. Pieces of wood and debris were strewn around him. At first, he did not see it, but there was a small chest that had fallen from that structure on the side of the mountain."

"Did you know that part of the story?" Jamil asked.

Heba motioned to him to stick his neck back in and watch.

"Okay, now Gaspar is picking up the story."

"The box contained scrolls from the time of Noah. They contained instructions for the celebration of the birth of the newborn King of the Jews."

He paused to let Mary and Joseph absorb what he was saying. Then he went on.

Jamil watched Mary set the sleeping baby down.

"The baby is in the manger," said Jamil.

Some of the other camels tried to peek over the top of Jamil.

"The scrolls told of the twelve spiritual gifts He would bring to humanity. These gifts are God's powers that are found in man when he recovers from his human condition and discovers his deep connection to the Divinity. When mankind fully realizes that we are made in God's image and we have access to virtue or spiritual power, then we are living our full potential."

"Now he is talking about spiritual power."

"Jamil, just listen for a while," said Heba.

"These twelve virtues are aspects of God's nature that are found in a man's soul," said Gaspar. "They were represented by different colored stones and were described in detail in the scrolls."

"Rarely does an individual develop his full potential and utilize these virtues," said Melchior. "Because of His Divine nature, this small baby will one day develop into a man who will fully manifest all twelve."

"When one turns inward and looks beyond the dark recesses of the mind, one finds the splendor of the soul and its God-given properties," said Gaspar. "These properties are spiritual gifts. We have chosen to bring Gold, Frankincense, and Myrrh. We bear gifts that represent these spiritual abilities or virtues."

There was a pause in the storytelling. Jamil, still on his knees, tried to move closer. He did not know how to explain these things to the other camels.

Gaspar nodded to Melchior, who stepped forward to speak. Jamil wanted to turn to Heba, but the youngest Magi was quick.

"We bring you Frankincense, called Olibanum, from Seba in the southern Arabian Peninsula. You use it in your temple during worship," said Melchior. "Frankincense represents the virtues of prudence, temperance, chastity, and Faith." He motioned to Merodak to come forward.

Bowing, he said, "I am Merodak, son of Bildad, and I bring you Frankincense in a jade bowl."

"It represents the virtue of prudence," he said and looked down at the baby. "Yours will be the power to make decisions with the will of God as the source of your decisiveness, little Yeshua." Merodak looked up at Mary and continued, "He will teach mankind how to discern the right use of one's resources and to use them for good and not evil."

Merodak brought a beautiful petite jade bowl with a lid that had a star carved on top. He handed the bowl to Mary, who lifted the lid to smell the Olibanum. Joseph, though only a carpenter, knew that Frankincense was precious.

The aroma was powerful. Jamil was glad when Mary carefully placed the lid back on top of the container. A camel's nose was much more sensitive than a man's.

Melchior motioned to Aksherosh, who moved toward the Holy family.

"This little jewel box is adorned with smoky Topaz, which symbolizes the divine virtue of temperance," said Aksherosh. "It is the virtue to say no to any temptation to do other than God's will and to live with moderation. It is the God-given ability to renounce self-defeating thoughts that lead us astray."

"I don't understand temperance, but I know about temptation," Jamil said.

"Your son's ability to resist temptation will enable him to resist the things of the world in exchange for his Father's kingdom. These smoky Topazes symbolize the beauty of his ability to be temperate." He handed the bejeweled box to Mary, and bowing, stepped back.

Melchior nodded to Sadlak, who stepped forward.

"Rubies are the color red," he said. "This is the color of the virtue of Chastity. Chastity is control of the power of life itself, and your son will use it for the benefit of humanity. He will awaken life in those who are willing to listen and be touched by him."

As Sadlak spoke, the baby Jesus looked into Mary's eyes. She stroked his head and said, "Jesus, listen closely to what these men have to say. They are talking about your heavenly Father's will for you."

"Sadlak is giving Joseph this beautiful little box," said Jamil.

The little camel was getting nervous now. His body twitched a muscle here and another there while trying to remain perfectly still. He nervously looked back at the other camels.

Melchior waited for Sadlak to return to his place. Solemnly, he approached the family with his gift of Frankincense. He held a brass pot with two side handles. On the front of the pot was the moon above Mount Ararat. It was made from a beautiful star sapphire.

"Royal blue represents the virtue of Faith," said Melchior. "This child shall walk by faith. His life will instill faith in God among the masses for all time. Faith is the

knowledge of things unseen. It is the God-given ability infused in man to believe in good and allow it to happen. Faith is the ability to carry out God's will, knowing that nothing can stand against it."

As Melchior handed the pot to Mary, Jesus stretched his hand out. She smiled as he gave a little grunt and then stared at Melchior.

Jamil suspected that it was probably a little air bubble from nursing, but he believed that the child understood. Even the star sapphire seemed to twinkle with His movement. Jesus was not interested in the gifts, but in the Magi. To Jamil, the baby already seemed wise enough to understand that the gift of Faith was far more valuable than the gift of Frankincense.

Melchior moved back to his group and Balthasar stepped forward.

"My group from Persia brings Myrrh, a fragrant resin that is used as a medicine and as a perfume," said the Magi Balthasar. "It symbolizes the virtues of zeal, fortitude, understanding, and hope."

"Akreho, son of Kesro, brings Myrrh in a container adorned with orange Topaz," said Akreho.

"Orange represents Zeal. It is the virtue of sustained enthusiastic action to carry out the will of God."

He presented Mary and Joseph with a diminutive marble box ornately decorated with orange Topaz. He moved to the back of the group just in front of Jamil.

The next Magi stepped forward.

"Arbakchest, son of Kolite, brings Myrrh in a box adorned with golden Topaz," said Balthasar.

"Arbakchest just got up and handed Joseph a box

studded with some kind of golden stone," reported Jamil to the others.

"Golden yellow Topaz represents the virtue Understanding," he said. "This babe will grow to a man of such understanding that all the secrets of the universe will be his to reveal." He bowed and stepped back.

"Astonkakodon, son of Sheshron, brings his offering of Myrrh in a container adorned with smoky Topaz," said Balthasar.

He stepped forward, bowed, and offered a small silver bowl with a lid covered with smokey, dark Topaz. "These dark jewels represent the virtue of Fortitude."

"You should see how beautiful this one is," whispered Jamil.

"His strength shall be that of the Creator's. His burdens, even if they may be many and great, will be lifted by a power so strong that the universe is sustained by it. Adversity will be the seed that causes his fortitude to be tested, drawn out, and enhanced."

Jamil watched the last gift of Myrrh from Balthasar himself, who announced, "I am Balthasar, son of Warzod of Persia. I bring Myrrh in a small chest of gold and silver adorned with Aquamarines.

"The Aquamarine represents the virtue of Hope. Their pale blue color represents the beauty of the sky. When Noah saw the blue of the sky, the hope that his family would survive was fulfilled and he knew that the ordeal was over. The rainbow was God's promise back to man."

"Your child will instill hope of eternal life to mankind, a hope that transcends even death itself."

Jamil started to say something to the others and then

thought better of it. *I am not going to even try to explain what that means.*

Mary took the gift. Balthasar bowed, and Gaspar stepped forward, stroked his beard, and smiled.

"From India, we bring gifts of Gold," Gaspar said. "Your son will never want, not because of his wealth, but because he will be as free of desire as the ancient sages of India. Gold represents the abundance of God, which shall be as evident in the accomplishments of His life as in the abundance of nature on Earth. Gold symbolizes the virtues of Forgiveness, Gratitude, Wisdom, and Love. Like Love, it is a substance that can not tarnish and is of value itself."

Gaspar spoke again. "Cosnasap, son of Gonapar, also brings Gold from India."

Jamil thought that Gaspar was looking at him. He was getting excited. He looked back at Heba and said, "Soon they will be speaking about me. I just know it."

Cosnasap stood and patted the camel on the brow. He approached Joseph with a small chest on a pillow of purple satin. On the chest was a huge Amethyst that matched the color of the cushion. The tiny chest was made of fine Oriental hardwood with gold clasps on the corners. He set the pillow and chest down with care.

"Purple symbolizes the virtue of Forgiveness," he said. "He will teach the power and wisdom of Forgiveness, which brings healing to all relationships and improves every situation. He will forgive the way his father in heaven forgives."

He brought his hands together over his heart, as was the Indian custom, then returned to his place.

Badadilma stepped forward.

"Dark green represents the virtue of Gratitude," said Badadilma. "Your child will have the ability to maintain Gratitude for everything in creation." He looked at the Child with love, "His life will overflow with peace and serenity because He will be able to see God's will in all that happens and be grateful."

When he stepped back, Hormidas stepped forward, nodding to Gaspar and bowing to Mary and Baby Jesus. He was a formidable man, dark and full-chested. He carried a small box with pale white silk trim. On top was a large pearl embedded in a mesh of fine gold, suspended by a small gold chain. He lifted the box and handed it to Joseph.

Jamil was certain the baby was looking at him.

"Pearl represents the virtue of Wisdom," said Hormidas. "Wisdom is the pearl of great value. It is the intuitive faculty of the mind, in tune with God's infinite intelligence. It creates good judgment in the minds of man. Your son will be blessed with infinite Wisdom. His every action will reflect the mind of God that adorns his frame. His Wisdom will astound the most learned teachers."

Jamil marveled at the Magi's wisdom. Soon it would be his turn to be a gift to the Child. His excitement suppressed his usual impatience.

Gaspar stepped forward. "I am Gaspar, son of Artiban, and I too, bring Gold from India."

He was a magnificent man, regal in stature and appearance. Jamil had never seen him look so grand. His flowing beard was as white as the silk that draped the small silver chest he carried. On top of the chest was a large square diamond that glimmered with reflected silver light. His old frame rose slowly.

"Hey, Massius. This is the gold you were carrying," Jamil whispered back.

Gaspar smiled at Mary and Joseph.

"Diamond symbolizes the virtue of Love. Love is God's true nature. It is the spirit of God moving through man that gives us the experience of love. Jesus will be so filled with love that he will be one with Love. In the oneness of that Love, great compassion will be given to the world. His heart is a sacred place of Love," said Gaspar. "His life is love and his mission is redemption."

Gaspar bowed, stepped back, and sat down.

Then Joseph spoke. "You have been generous beyond anything we could have dreamed of. On behalf of my wife and child, I humbly accept these gifts."

"You have blessed us with an abundance that we did not expect," said Mary. "Please pray with me for the wisdom to use it wisely."

The ceremony was over. The men stood up to leave.

I thought I was to be given to the child. Wasn't I supposed to? Where did I get that idea from? Jamil thought to himself.

He let himself be led out of the stable. His head hung low, confused, and disappointed. He was too upset to bother fighting with Abdul.

* * *

After the Magi presented the gifts to the Holy Family, the camel drivers went outside to set up camp. They helped themselves to the bread and wine and toasted to the little Child. They were preparing to spend the night encamped in a field outside the stable. Abdul and Nemir

were in a jovial mood, entertaining themselves at the expense of the others. They tried not to make too much noise because the baby was sleeping in the distance. At a certain point, the camel drivers were invited to meet the Child.

Nemir immediately fussed over the baby. His childlike attitude was endearing. He naturally mentioned to Mary that Abdul's wife was expecting. When he predicted a boy this time, the other men laughed.

Mary smiled.

"First, let his wife and the new baby be healthy," she said. "Let it be God's choice what it will be, but hopefully a boy."

She laughed, then turned to Abdul and prayed aloud for a boy. The evening grew darker and Jesus was put to sleep in his manger, which was now surrounded by small gifts adorned with jewels. Jesus was the priceless treasure in the center.

The men left to finish making their camp. Gaspar, Balthasar, and Melchior walked outside with Joseph. With them was the camel, Jamil, who carried that strange pack.

"Joseph," said Gaspar, "We were commanded in a dream to build this thing and mount it on this camel's back."

"What sort of device is that?" asked Joseph.

"We have used it to carry our yogurt on this journey, but have not been certain about its true purpose," said Balthasar.

"This camel with the pack is the last gift we bring. We were hoping that you would understand what it was for," said Gaspar.

Mary walked out to see what the men were talking

about. She took one look at Jamil and said, "A baby saddle and supply pack. How lovely." She added, "See, right here is where the legs go."

The men started to mutter. It now seemed obvious about the pack's purpose.

Joseph cautiously approached the other camels. Livestock was valuable, but he had never been fond of camels. They were temperamental animals and of no use to a carpenter. He was much more content with a donkey and would have enjoyed the use of a horse.

Mary did not particularly like the odor of the camels either. They were different from the animals that she was familiar with. However, she did appreciate the luxurious fabric that covered Jamil and his saddle. She reached up to touch the starburst blaze on his head.

Jamil was a little edgy and suddenly moved, startling Mary and causing her to jump. When the men realized that she was unharmed, they laughed.

"The animal is yours for the child's use," said Gaspar. "He is quite gentle."

"I think not," said Mary, her eyes growing wide. "The child does not need a camel at this time."

Balthasar knew that she refused the gift because she had been startled.

Balthasar turned to Joseph to offer the camel to him, but Mary's eyes implored him not to accept it. Joseph tried to refuse it politely. It was difficult to be gracious and refuse at the same time. He really could not see any use for the animal. It would take time and work to care for it and groom it properly. He wasn't sure he could do either well.

"Think it over tonight," said Gaspar. "We would rather not bring the animal back with us to Persia."

Gaspar was gracious. He wished to spare Mary and Joseph any embarrassment. He faced Balthasar. "A mother always understands the needs of her child better than a man can. Perhaps we shall withdraw this gift."

Psalm 27:14
"Wait for the LORD with courage;
be stouthearted, and wait for the LORD."

15

THE REJECTION OF JAMIL

The disappointed Jamil was led away by Abdul.

"Don't worry, little one, I still think that you are a terrific gift. You just scared her. She will reconsider and tell the Magi that she wants you."

Nemir came over and helped Abdul pull the child-seat off the camel. They gently set it down and started to groom the animal. When they finished, they tethered him to Heba and went back to sit down with the others.

The silence was awkward. Jamil spoke first.

"Nice trip. I'm brought all the way out here to be a baby chair carrier and I get 'no thanks' for all my trouble."

Heba wanted to be supportive.

"Wait until the morning. I am sure they will want to take you," she said.

"I doubt it."

"This is just another example of being powerless over something. You have no control over what the good woman will do. So why be concerned?"

"Why be concerned? Why be concerned that I have been dragged hundreds of miles with a bundle of rags on my back, on a caravan that I didn't want to be a part of? Why be concerned that I have been forced to endure hardship in the desert and all for rejection?"

"Rejection is a hard thing to take."

Jamil was silent.

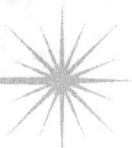

"This was harder on you than I thought," said Heba.

Silence. Just a look.

"You must want to be accepted by this Holy Family."

"It's not about being accepted by this family, Heba. It's about living a meaningless life. I've walked all over the Sustainer's earth and I've gone nowhere."

Jamil took a breath and looked around. When Heba did not respond, he went on.

"I could have stayed at the oasis of Kashan and continued to eat, drink, and race other camels. At least I would have enjoyed myself."

"Would you really?" asked Heba. "Or would you be miserable, with no purpose in life, but to live at the oasis?"

"As long as I have to lead a miserable life, I may as well be at an oasis."

Jamil was frustrated. He swung his head to and fro, thinking. An idea was struggling to be born.

"No, that's not it at all," said Jamil. "I hoped that this journey would give me some answers about my purpose."

"Your purpose, Jamil, is to discover the Sustainer's will for you."

"Sounds great. Then what happens?"

"Then your life is serene and filled with boundless confidence. You have unlimited energy to carry out the tasks of life. Your confidence will not be based on appearances, but on the knowledge that God's plan is unfolding," Heba counseled.

"Serene ... boundless confidence ... You make it sound so wonderful."

"It is."

"I doubt I'll ever know."

"I can tell you how you will know," said Heba.

"Give me the simple version, for slow camels."

Heba smiled. She knew that his sarcasm was covering up a desire to know the truth. "First, you must admit that you are powerless over your natural camel instincts."

"I know that part already."

"When you do, you will find yourself in pain. Then you must be willing to let go of your desire to use anything but the Sustainer to heal your pain."

"I didn't use anything to heal my pain. As you can see, I'm stuck in it," said Jamil.

She said nothing, letting him sit in his pain. His disappointment mounted.

"I let you convince me to come on this crazy voyage. I've traveled for weeks through scorching heat and over dry sand, carrying a silly burden. I was hoping that somehow, I would find my purpose," Jamil said.

"You may in the morning. The key is that you must believe that finding God's purpose for you will ease your pain," said Heba. "You must keep believing that the Sustainer can give you meaning, not anything else."

Heba's big eyes looked directly into Jamil's. She could see something in him was resisting mightily.

"Part of me doesn't believe that one hundred percent."

"Before you can develop a sense of purpose, you must be willing to completely trust God with two things."

"What two?" asked Jamil.

"Your life and your will," said Heba.

"What does that mean? This sounds like becoming a mindless, spineless fool who doesn't do anything on his own," said Jamil.

"No," said Heba.

"Do I sit around and do nothing, expecting the Sustainer to take care of it all?"

"No," she answered again.

"Well, I don't get it."

"You cannot get this one with your head. It is not an intellectual process. It is intuitive," said Heba.

He thought about that. *She was right. Thinking did not work.*

"You must go deep inside, away from the turmoil of your thoughts, and ask for understanding."

"And then?" asked Jamil.

"And then you take action to do what you believe the Sustainer wants you to do."

"Let's suppose I decide to do something. What is the guarantee that it will work out?" asked Jamil.

"There is none," Heba said.

"There is none! I can make my own mistakes without all this effort!" he cried.

"Yes, you could."

"I could do a lot of things without always questioning what the Sustainer wants me to do. Life was much simpler back at the oasis."

"You can never go back to a time when life was simpler," said Heba. "You can only simplify how life is lived from here on."

"There you go again with those mysterious sayings that have so much meaning." His voice was filled with frustration.

"You are baffled because you cannot understand God's will. Next, you will be irritable because you were hoping that the riddle of life would be solved."

"Yeah, I want to understand the riddle of life," Jamil said. His tone was a little less serious.

"Small riddle? Easy answers?"

"Okay, big riddle, but I still don't get half of what you are trying to teach me."

"If you get only half of what I am trying to teach you, then I am satisfied," said Heba.

"I still don't get why you are giving me a hard time about being rejected by Mary."

"No matter how good a reason you have for feeling bad, it still is not good enough. When you have a tremendous belief that God is taking care of the outcome of your life, there are no good reasons, just excuses," said Heba.

"If I had no excuses, that would really limit me."

"No matter how bad it looks . . . no excuses, only hope."

"Are you telling me not to be upset about Mother Mary not wanting me as a gift for her son, Jesus? Of all the gifts of the Magi, I am the only one not accepted and I should not be hurt by that?"

"That's right, Jamil," said Heba. "Don't be upset. Be grateful, because God's plan will be far better than that which disappoints you."

"You make it sound like trying to make something good happen for me is getting in the way of something better."

Heba raised her large eyebrows and smiled. He was getting it.

* * *

Back at Caesarea Maritima, the four Roman Auxilia dismounted at the Hasmoneam Palace and quickly walked in. Herod looked up as they entered, then brushed aside the

people in his court. He motioned for the guards to come closer.

When alone, he asked the cavalrymen, "Tell me what happened with them?"

"They were honest," said the first cavalryman. "They went directly to the town of Bethlehem. There cannot be more than a few children in the area who are the right age."

"And you left as soon as you arrived at the outskirts of town to avoid suspicion?" asked Herod.

"No one suspected a thing," said the cavalryman.

"Good," said Herod. "We must allow them to think we will honor the child. These wise men, what fools. Did any of you discover the true nature of their mission? I must know what they had planned."

Herod was thinking about a possible plot by the Zealots of Israel to overthrow him. He was the King, not by God's ordination, but by Imperial proclamation.

The Auxilia were thinking practically, not politically.

"Perhaps," said the second cavalryman, as he stepped forward, "I have an idea about that strange device on the back hump of the camel, sir."

"What was it?" asked Herod.

"A special device to carry the child."

Herod mused for a while. The idea that the Magi would try to take the child with them was a really bad one. If the child were to leave and then return as a young man, nurtured by these wealthy Orientals, there would be no telling what would happen.

"Are there any Jewish settlements in Arabia and Persia, or India?" Herod asked,

The third Auxila, who was the Roman expert on Judaism

and other so-called Eastern Cults, cleared his throat. He was a doting intellectual whom Herod disliked but needed to manage Judea.

"There are settlements in all those places. During the census, we found that there were Jews as far away as Srinigar in Northern India," he said.

"We must be careful not to let the child leave Judea," said Herod. "When they come back to Jerusalem, we will pay tribute to the child and then accompany the Magi to the borders of the Roman Empire. The child will not leave the Empire of Caesar alive. I promise you that."

"Sir, would it not be wise to station some soldiers near the town of Bethlehem to watch their movements?" asked the last priest.

"And let them understand our intentions? You fool!" stormed Herod.

The Auxilia cowered before him. Herod could be deadly when enraged.

"We must be extremely careful. Caesar will not burn his foot on this star. I swear by the gods, he won't!"

Herod was in a rage as the Auxilia exited. He paced the room and brooded over how he would order the baby killed.

Matthew 2:12
*"And having been warned in a dream
not to return to Herod, they departed for their country
by another way."*

16

SOUTH TO BEERSHEBA

A great light descended from the sky and filled the crater.

"Makhtesh Ramon," a mighty voice intoned. Jamil trembled.

Great waters swirled into the crater, carving marks into the gypsum. The great chalk walls hung like white vestments on the loins of the Sustainer.

Then he heard the immense voice reverberate, "Makhtesh Ramon, you were given to Isaac and Jacob. You were given this arid land that you may receive my blessings. My gifts are many. None may keep the fulfillment of my promises from you."

He awoke with a start.

"Jamil, did you have a restless sleep?" asked Heba.

"My God, what a dream! The air was filled with howling winds and piercing sand. Then there was a great light, floods of water, and an overwhelming voice. It was scary."

"No need for fear," said Heba. "The Sustainer sends us our dreams so we can understand more fully the bountiful nature of his grace."

"If that was the Sustainer speaking to me, then I don't want to know his wrath," said Jamil.

It was early morning, and the Magi were in a circle, discussing the strange forms and features of their dreams. These princes spent their lives studying the signs of God

as revealed in dreams. Last night was important. Gaspar revealed that a yellow light in his dream blocked the road from Bethlehem to Jerusalem.

"Prudence would not have us return to Jerusalem. It is our solemn duty to follow this direction," said Gaspar.

"What of our promise to tell Herod of the baby's exact location upon our return to Jerusalem?" asked Balthasar.

"We must listen to the will of the light of the universe. It has spoken clearly in my dream," said Gaspar.

"This is a grave situation," said Melchior. "I too had a dream instructing me to go elsewhere."

"What was your dream?" asked Balthasar.

"From the sea of Galilee down the Jordan River flowed a stream of blood. I traveled south to a well. There, a man known as Isaac took an oath and offered seven baby lambs for peace. Then he walked into the desert to wait."

A murmur rippled through the group. They started talking to each other. Some nodded, while others gesticulated their obviously different opinions.

The Sea of Galilee flowed down the Jordan through the Jordan Valley and into the Dead Sea. It was surrounded by the wilderness of Judea. The geography of Melchior's dream was easy to interpret until the mention of the well and the oath. The Magi vigorously debated the various meanings of the well. They did not understand Isaac, but the peace offering of the seven lambs meant that this was once a battlefield and an oath of peace had been taken there.

The Magi did not come to any conclusion on the meaning of the dream. But now even Balthasar was certain they were not to return to Jerusalem.

"My sleep was not tranquil. I was aroused by a vision. The silver light of God spoke to me. It said, 'Throw two camels into my white-sided well. Give not this gift to the Child.'"

All eyes were on Balthasar, waiting for him to continue.

"I asked the light where I should find this white-sided well. And the light said, 'Next to the land of Mohab.'"

"It is clear that we must travel south and not north to Jerusalem," said Gaspar. "Let us prepare to depart."

Joseph noticed the activity in the camp. He helped Mary up so she could see what was going on. With baby Jesus in her arms, she watched the men packing. His eyes were in rapt attention on her face. Then He looked at the camp. She imagined that the little Child looked right at Jamil.

"Jamil, I think the Divine One likes you," Heba said.

"Maybe today I will be accepted as the last gift from the Magi."

Jamil felt better already. When Joseph approached the Magi, Jamil's spirits soared. He was going to be the personal mount for this child of wonder.

"Now is the time to be patient, little one," said Heba. "We must learn to take victory and defeat, good and bad, honor and travail, with the same state of mind. Be patient and trust that God's will is being expressed at this moment."

"I see you are preparing to depart," said Joseph, who was holding the baby for them to see. "When will you leave?"

"This morning we will go back to our lands in the East," said Gaspar.

The Holy Family marveled at how quickly the camel drivers were able to pack and load the animals. Abdul and Nemir showed Joseph how to load around the animal's hump.

"Some say the humps are filled with water, but it is their stomach that swells when you let them drink too much," said Abdul.

"There is not a finer animal to ride over the desert," said Nemir.

He motioned to the young camel with the device.

"Come, put the child in the seat. Let us see how well it fits him," he said.

Mary shook her head no, but Joseph walked over with the child.

"Here, let us see how well it was shaped."

Joseph was enjoying the fun, and Jesus did not seem to mind. He stretched and yawned. It looked like he was reaching out toward the camel.

"Please, Joseph, be careful," Mary said.

"This little animal has been specially trained to walk briskly without rocking from side to side just for you, little Baby," he said to Jesus.

Gaspar, Melchior, and Balthasar walked over with the Holy Family. Gaspar watched as Joseph gently held the child near the seat. Jesus appeared to be much too small. He stepped back and smiled.

"Too small, I guess. How do you get on?"

Nemir held the reins of the animal while Abdul mounted it, to show how one sits on a camel. With the seat in place, it was relatively easy for a driver to sit on top and between the two humps.

Mary was not enjoying any of this, but Joseph appreciated fine livestock. He stood next to the camel, holding Jesus carefully. The little camel remained perfectly still.

Gaspar turned to Mary. He saw her distress.

"We withdraw this gift from our offerings to your child. We hope that does not offend you."

Mary smiled in relief.

"You should do whatever you think God wants you to do. We will not be disappointed."

Abdul turned Jamil around, away from Mary and Joseph.

"We are heading south, as we have been instructed in our dreams," said Balthasar. "We have been told not to leave this beast with you, but to deliver these two to a white-sided well, possibly for a sacrifice or ritual of some sort."

Mary was horrified at the thought of harming the animals.

Melchior read it on her face.

"It is not as you would think. We will not harm the animals, but they are to be given up in some way at a white-sided well of God."

"What could that be?" asked Mary.

"We are not sure," said Melchior. "We hoped you and your husband could help us with the interpretation of a dream."

"How could we possibly help you?" asked Joseph. "We are not trained in the interpretation of dreams like our ancestor Joseph did for the Pharaoh."

"But this dream is a mystery to us," said Melchior. "We must head south to a land where Isaac made an oath at a well. It was a land where a battle was fought."

"We do not know who Isaac is either," added Balthasar.

"Isaac is not a mystery," said Joseph. "Isaac was a descendent of Abraham, who fought the Philistines. Abraham made a peace offering of seven lambs and took an oath to maintain the peace. This was at the last well, just before the entrance to the Negev desert in the south. The town is called Beersheba. Beer means well and sheba means oath."

The Magi looked at each other. Their understanding was dawning.

"Then it was Isaac who made the town of Beersheba into what it is today?" asked Melchior.

He wondered why Isaac had headed into the desert and waited after the seven lambs were offered in peace.

"Yes," said Joseph, "But it was Abraham who took the oath."

"Either way, we should head toward the town of Beersheba," said Gaspar. He listened to this bit of Jewish history. It explained Melchior's dream.

The men finished, and the caravan was reassembled.

Mary was sitting with Jesus in her arms, and Joseph was standing next to them. They bid the Magi farewell as the caravan moved off from the stable back into town. The Magi were going to take the main road south. It would take an almost entire day of travel to reach Beersheba.

Joseph went off to register for the census. Before he found his way to the synagogue, he walked to the inn to purchase some food. The wife of the innkeeper treated him kindly and refused payment. She only wanted to tend to Mary and help her through the first days. She offered to bring food back to Mary and look in on her while he

was registering. She promised them that tonight would be their last in the stable because some of the travelers were leaving in the morning.

Matthew 2:14
"Joseph rose and took the child and his mother by night and departed for Egypt."

17
THE CHASE BEGINS

Joseph woke with a start. In the middle of the night, an angel appeared in a dream. The message was clear.

"You must flee immediately to Egypt. The child is in danger."

He was so disturbed by the dream that he roused Mary.

"We must leave," he said. "We must leave at once!"

"Joseph, what happened?" she asked, alarmed by his tone.

"An angel came to me in a dream and told me that we must leave. I fear the baby's life is in danger."

"Then we must go at once," she said.

Mary was a woman of faith. She knew that the angel would not have appeared to her, as it had at the well, to announce she was with child. She was now part of a family. The angel appeared to the head of the household, respecting Jewish customs.

Mary quickly packed provisions for her family. There was no telling how long it would take them to travel to Egypt. Perhaps they would head to Leontopolis, where there was a large Jewish population and a temple rivaling that of Solomon. The Jewish settlements near the Nile were numerous. There was a thriving trade along these routes. A journey to Leontopolis took between two and three days, but she was weak from childbirth and would not be able to move quickly. If they were fleeing danger,

though, the trip could take longer because they might have to hide.

Mary looked at the donkey's hard saddle and was worried. It would be a blessing to have the camel with its plush seat right now. She also realized that her husband would have to walk. The Holy Family had one donkey, but during the night, they would not be able to purchase another. The trip would be slowed down because they did not accept that little camel. She continued to throw things together and decided it was no use fretting.

In the meantime, Joseph packed the gifts from the Magi. They were mostly small jewel boxes that he rolled into their blankets. He packed them carefully on the donkey. He was not sure how long they would have to remain in Egypt. They might need to become anonymous. He would have to use the treasures from the Magi, carefully.

* * *

The Magi arrived in the town of Beersheba the previous afternoon. It had been much easier than they had expected because of the Roman fanaticism toward building roads. They sat quietly, trying to unravel the mystery of Isaac going into the desert to wait and the riddle of the white-sided well. It was easier than they anticipated. The answers came to them out of the blue.

Abdul and Nemir were sent to town to buy feed for the camels. The Magi stayed on the outskirts, careful not to attract attention. While in town, Nemir spoke to one of the Jewish merchants.

"I hear tell that your fine city was founded by Abraham himself," said Nemir.

"It was," said the merchant, eyeing his customer closely. He was hard-pressed to determine the status of the man before him, making it difficult for him to price the items. Was this a servant of a wealthy man or a moderately successful businessman? He would like to be able to charge a little extra, and could if the man's master was rich.

"Abraham's oath at the well is what this city is," said the merchant proudly. "Isaac and Jacob both lived here."

"Is the well here?" asked Nemir.

"It is in the center of town. I will take you to it if you like," said the merchant. A short tour might insure a large tip.

"I would like to draw water from it. I hear it could bring me good fortune."

"That it would," said the merchant.

Abdul listened to the two men and decided to join in.

"Well, my friend, Nemir, you will be able to tell that soon-to-be-born son of yours that you drank at the white-sided well of Isaac for good luck."

"He should not do that," said the merchant. "The white-sided well of Isaac has not brought anyone luck, ever. That is a different well, and it is located in Negev, a few miles from here."

"It's not the same well?" asked Abdul.

"No, it is not even a well. It is a bizarre basin that was carved out of the desert. Isaac liked to go off into the desert to be alone with God. The real name of the place is Makhtesh Ramon."

"Why is it known as the white-sided well?" asked Nemir, who was amazed at how easy it was to find the riddle's answer.

"Because Isaac used to go there to drink in the divine. The walls of the canyon are made of gypsum and chalk, pure white like the garments of a rich virgin bride," said the merchant.

The merchant accompanied the camel drivers to the well at Beersheba. He bid them a good journey. He received a great tip too.

* * *

Another day had dawned on the city of Jerusalem. Herod had grown impatient waiting for the Magi to return. If the Magi did not reappear by that evening, he had decided to send soldiers to Bethlehem. He would send only a few to not arouse suspicion.

He already had ordered that travelers from the town be questioned about the arrival of the Magi. Yesterday's reports verified that the Magi had spent the night camped off in a small field on the outskirts of town. Today's reports would verify any movement by the Magi.

A Jewish king was a great concern to Herod. He was suspicious of anyone who might succeed him. He was even jealous of his sons. He had become so wary of his sons' ambitions that he had several put to death. This did not simplify matters much, since he had nine wives and twenty-seven children. His true mistress was death. It was his political companion. He smiled fondly as he reminisced about his brother Phasael's death, an alleged suicide. It had been an involuntary suicide, known as murder to most people. That was a time when Herod's life was much simpler. All he had to do was orchestrate one death and Samaria was his to administer with Judea. These were more

complicated times. The Zealots wanted him overthrown and were awaiting a Messiah. The Pharisees did not trust him because he did not follow the Jewish law properly. He did not need matters complicated by contending with a true Jewish King, from the House of David.

Herod thought about the Parthian uprising that occurred just before he came to power. At that time, he had to get the Roman Senate's backing to put down the uprising. Things did not cool off until he married the Parthian king's daughter. He had to dispose of some of her children who did not like him. By comparison, this Jewish heir to the throne should be easy. This was a baby he was contending with.

First, he thought, *I must know who I am to kill. The killing is easy. It is like killing an animal for a sacrifice. They have no idea what you are about to do. Lambs even lick your hand. They deserve to be killed for being so stupid, so vulnerable.*

He licked his lips in anticipation.

The hunt was not for blood, but for power. Who would control the greater portion of the Roman land? If you controlled it all, like Augustus, you were considered a god. He had fought for a long time to control what he had, and he was not letting one hectare of it go. Power gave him incredible wealth. He could tax at will, and in a moment, decide how much he would bleed from these greedy people. Wealth gave him control over people. He liked that. He needed that. He had nine wives because he liked to control the women he was near. He was blind to his greed for money, land, and women.

In the next few days, Herod needed to control one

more life. He looked out over the balcony and the city of Jerusalem.

"Nothing in the world can stop me, Little Child. You will be crushed by me. I am Herod the Great and I control the destinies of men."

He laughed as he continued to stare out over the city.

* * *

Jamil was still carrying the contraption on his back. He thought it was idiotic that they continued to make him carry that load.

"Heba," he said, "I think men are fools."

"Why do you say that, my little friend?"

"The Magi are supposed to be the most brilliant of the lot. Yet, they are making me keep this thing on my back and we are still walking all over God's creation. It makes no sense to me."

"But they are brilliant, Jamil," said Heba.

"Sure, and on a few threads of dreams, they walk us toward a desert, which will make our journey that much more difficult to endure."

"Trust the Sustainer. Everything is going to turn out perfectly," said Heba.

"Perfect for what?" asked Jamil.

"Perfect for your spiritual growth," said Heba. "It may not turn out as you would like it to, but the Sustainer is going to put all the pieces together so you can grow from your personal adversities."

"Are you saying that I can't fail?"

"You can't fail to grow spiritually if you trust in the Sustainer," said Heba.

"None of the stuff you tell me says I'll be okay physically," said Jamil.

"None of what I say is for you to use to succeed on a material plane, though you could use it for physical survival. It is for your spiritual growth. It is to be used to discover your purpose, which somehow is to be an instrument of God's will."

"I thought you told me that discovering my life's purpose won't make me happy?" asked Jamil. "Isn't that what you said the other day?"

"That is correct," said Heba. "Discovering your life's purpose will not make you happy, but living it will."

"What's the difference?"

"Discovering it means you know what you have got to do. Living it means walking the walk of faith, even in things unseen, because you know that the Sustainer's plan for you is better than any plan you could make up for yourself."

"Thus far, I have been dragged around in an almost mindless manner. Humans are like that. I have learned that I can do without water, though I still love it so much, and I am working on it one step at a time and one day at a time. Oh, and I'm grateful that I was born a camel and not a horse. But have I learned much else?"

Jamil was bantering with Heba to see where he could push the debate. He felt like a little argument would be fun. The travel was so effortless for him that he did not have to think about it.

"You would be surprised at how much you have learned, Jamil," said Heba.

"I don't feel wiser, just more confused."

Jamil knew she could not argue against his confusion. It was a purely subjective experience.

"Just because you feel confused about certain things, does not mean that you haven't learned. Confusion is a sure sign that you are learning."

Darn, she has an answer for everything. "Here we go again. How is confusion a sure sign that I am learning?" asked Jamil. *I think you're crazy, but I'm not going to say it out loud.*

"There are three phases to mastering something. First, you get the overall picture of what it is you do not know. This feels like excitement or discovery. Then you learn. The learning phase feels like confusion until the last phase, mastery. Mastery feels like you know it. So, if you tell me that you feel confused by what I say, I assume that you are learning something."

Jamil was confused all right. *I must be learning . . . and maybe she's not so crazy.*

"And once I feel as though I have mastered the subject, that means that I have stopped learning?" Jamil asked.

"Precisely," said Heba. "No longer learning is not a negative. It simply is the last phase, mastery."

"Once I have learned it and know it, then I have mastery, as you call it?" asked Jamil. *I think I'm actually getting this.*

"Not completely. You have complete mastery when you put what you know into action repeatedly. Then a strange thing happens. You can sit back and watch your body do that which you have mastered. It becomes effortless. You become the silent observer of the process. Now, that is what I call mastery."

"You have broken this thing down into its phases, haven't you?" he asked.

Jamil was thinking about how effortless running was. It was the only example that came to his mind.

"It becomes clearer every time I teach it," said Heba. "Let me give you an example. First, you realized there was a new skill, walking in the desert one step at a time, smooth and simple, and that we are powerless over our desire for water. You know the principles. Then you arrived at a point where all you felt was confusion, frustration, and pain."

"Yes, I remember that part quite well."

"Then the process started to make sense. It even seemed simple. Not that you were enjoying it, but at least you had a hold of what it meant to be a camel and to let the Sustainer's will work for you. Thus far, you have not been able to surrender completely. When that happens, it becomes a dance with the divine, almost effortless and serene. That is coming, Jamil, and when it does, you will know the difference."

"I'd like to get to the point where I'm serene, doing all the things a camel in the desert needs to do," said Jamil. He meant it. He wanted serenity.

"Like I said, soon. All you need is to get to a point where your total existence is threatened."

Total existence threatened? Is she crazy, or am I?

"Where life becomes so unmanageable that you make a conscious choice to turn your life over to the care of the Sustainer. Then it happens."

"What happens?" asked Jamil

"Something deep down changes and you can never go

back to who you were before. You may not understand what to do, but something inside knows intuitively."

"I don't know how to do that," said Jamil.

"You don't have to know how. You just have to be willing. In matters of the spirit, willingness is more important than knowing how."

Heba looked around. They were coming into rougher terrain. This was the famed Negev Desert.

"From the stories I have heard, it is not a wonderful place to wander around in," said Jamil

The little one shuddered. He had heard the stories; Winds that could be fierce for hours, and grains of gypsum and chalk that made the dryness feel even worse. Even a camel struggled in this environment.

Abdul and Nemir took the reins of the two camels and walked them out in front of the rest of the caravan. The Magi looked at the beasts and nodded to each other. Balthasar handed a bolt of fine white linen fabric to Abdul.

"Place this in the child's seat to support him so that they may travel more quickly."

As Abdul complied, Gaspar spoke to Nemir.

"It is only right that we leave the older one with the younger one. They have grown attached to each other."

The two camel drivers nodded in agreement.

Melchior ordered one of the camel drivers to change the pack on the older animal. They prepared a change in equipment and strung extra water gourds on the side. The new pack was set up with a saddle.

Balthasar was getting the men to cover the baby-carrying device with a rough, but durable cloth.

"We do not know how long the beasts will be out here.

Make sure it is on tight and that there isn't a possibility it will blow off."

Gaspar addressed Nemir and Abdul. "Just over the rise, you will see a basin carved into the desert floor. It extends as far as the eye can see."

"Makhtesh Ramon?" asked Nemir.

"The white-sided well of Isaac," said Gaspar. "You must get the two camels into the basin. Get far enough away so that they will not be able to follow you out."

"Where will you be, sir, when we get back?" asked Abdul.

"We will head directly east, toward the land of Mohab. You will have to push your animals to catch up with us. If you do not catch us in the first eight hours, take this small medallion to the city of Kir-Mohab and ask for the high priest at the temple. He will supply you with the proper provisions to return to the Baghdad region."

"We wish you God speed in your journey," said Balthasar.

"Remember, you must get them into the basin before you leave," said Melchior.

"May the light of Faith lead you on your path."

With that, Gaspar turned his mount around and the others followed suit.

Jamil turned to Heba. His fear was palpable.

"Did you hear that?" he asked. "They're going to drop us into the basin known as Makhtesh Ramon."

Jamil was panicking, and Heba knew it. He didn't care if she knew.

"That was the name of the place in my dream. We are going to be used in some sort of animal sacrifice. We should run away right now."

"No, Jamil. We must face what we fear."

Though Heba's voice was calm, he was having trouble feeling reassured.

"You believe this whole thing is going to work out?"

He was gravely concerned.

"Jamil, after all you have been through, do you believe that the Sustainer has brought you this far just to drop you into a well? Do you think God will toss you away?"

"You have a point. God wouldn't just let me go, abandon me, after all this."

He was trying to convince himself that this was true but he feared God would abandon him.

"Of course not, Jamil," said Heba.

"But this place was mentioned in my dream. I fear it. I'll not be stranded there. It's barren, desolate, and very scary."

"You know this for a fact, and yet you have never even been there."

As the camels talked, the two men continued to lead them over the slight rise in the terrain. They approached the top and then stopped. Before them was a basin so vast as to be almost unimaginable. There were gigantic strips of chalk running hundreds of feet long down the mighty walls. It was a stark contrast to the gray gypsum and brown rock. Everywhere that the eye could see were rock formations that had been carved by the water of a current that must have been very swift and violent.

Jamil grew more and more unsettled. As he approached the great basin, his mind kept wandering back to the dream. How was this infertile land part of the fulfillment of the Sustainer's promises to Isaac?

The camels moved close to the edge of the basin. There was a small path that led precipitously down to the floor of the basin. It wound around and then made hairpin turns and dove further into the vast abyss, clinging to the chalk walls. When Jamil saw the path, he came to a halt. He couldn't move. The path was too steep. The turns were too sharp. He would never be able to walk down. He panicked. Heba stopped too. Camels were not fit for this kind of terrain. It was meant for a mule or a mountain goat. The only reason it was fit for a camel was that it was dry.

Abdul climbed down from his mount, walked over to Heba, and placed a cloth above her eyes. He had a Zoroastrian cap that had two felt pads on the sides. He bent them forward to create tunnel vision for the animal and repeated the process on Jamil. The younger camel was then tied behind Heba to her saddle. He pulled on Heba's reins, but the little camel in the back refused to move.

"Switch them around and put the little one in front. He will obey you better with your hand on his reins," Nemir shouted.

Abdul made the switch. He checked everything one more time. He noticed the bolt of white cloth in the baby's chair was sticking up. He tucked it down tight so it would not hit the wall as they walked.

Nemir was off his mount and stood near the edge, looking over. He stayed behind to hold their own camels. Nemir watched for what seemed like an eternity until Abdul reached the bottom of the basin.

Abdul pulled the two caps off. He looked at the bolt of linen and realized it was too large for the baby. He pulled it

out. Then he put both caps in the baby seat. That seemed about right. He hefted the linen over his shoulder. He figured he would have to bring it back to the Magi.

Abdul climbed back up the cliff. By the time he trudged all the way to the top, he was out of breath.

"Let us wait to see if they can climb out on their own, or if they are trapped down in that Godforsaken place," Abdul said.

Nemir spotted the bolt of cloth and asked, "Why didn't you leave it?"

"I didn't think it would fit," he said. "Here, strap it on your camel. You have more room."

"Couldn't you have strapped it on one of the camels down there and left it?"

"I wasn't thinking. And I'm not going back down."

Nemir shrugged and then attached it to the back of his saddle.

They waited for a few minutes while they checked their packs and prepared to leave in pursuit of the Magi. The whole ordeal had taken a little more than an hour, so they knew that they were only a few miles behind the caravan.

When they started to pull away, they noticed that Jamil was struggling desperately to climb back up, while the older camel seemed content to stay in the white-sided well. Jamil could not climb out by himself, because Heba was tied to his back. The two of them could not climb back up, side by side, because the hill was too steep and the path too narrow. The old camel was not ready to leave.

Jamil said to Heba, "Experience greatness . . . camel . . . stop drinking . . . caravan journey."

There was a decidedly sarcastic tone in his voice.

* * *

The Beersheba marketplace was reopening after the midday meal. Joseph and Mary walked into town, obviously fatigued after many hours of travel. Baby Jesus was awake. He had slept most of the journey, awakening only to be fed. They needed to find a safe haven for a short period of time where they could rest and perhaps find another donkey.

Joseph had a distant cousin here in town and hoped to stop for a short while at their home. They had traveled under the sun and were very weak. It was not wise to be out in this climate during the middle of the day, especially with Mary.

After resting under a palm tree and feeding the baby, Mary looked at the stands in the marketplace for some food to take with them. They did not want to be a burden on their relatives. While she walked from stand to stand looking at fruits and nuts, Joseph listened for any news that might be relevant to their flight. As far as he could tell, no one was looking for them. They were treated merely as travelers passing through. The couple made discreet inquiries about their relatives and then headed toward the south side of town.

Psalm 50:15
"Then call upon me in time of distress;
I will rescue you and you shall glorify me."

18

STORM IN THE NEGEV

As night fell on Jerusalem, Herod put down his cup of wine and walked out onto the balcony. Still, no word came from Bethlehem as to whether the Magi had departed yet.

He anxiously awaited their return. He tried to imagine the feast that he would give on their arrival. For some reason, he was having trouble. *They would be impressed*, he thought, trying to convince himself. He hoped that the Zoroastrians would welcome his hospitality. This afternoon, Herod let it be known that he would like to have some of his favorite belly dancers at the meal. While he fantasized about which of his nine wives would be present, a centurion entered the chamber.

"Sir, we have received news that the Zoroastrians have left Bethlehem," said the young Gaius Cassius known as Longinus, a Roman Centurion.

"What time will they arrive?" he asked.

"They left yesterday and have not reached Jerusalem yet, sir," said the centurion.

He watched closely for signs of Herod's fury, which was known to blow as viciously as a winter storm. No one in Judea wished to be the target of his wrath.

Herod was strangely calm as he walked back out to the balcony. A few sparrows flew off, wise to leave him alone.

"Do we have any reports of where they have gone?" he asked.

"They may have gone south toward Beersheba," he said.

"What evidence do you have? Be specific," said Herod.

The centurion called to one of the guards, who ushered in a terrified peasant to stand before Herod. With a faint smile, Herod addressed the man.

"Good fellow, don't be alarmed." He paused and asked, "Have you, perchance, seen a magnificent caravan of travelers from the East?"

The peasant nodded.

"Speak up peasant," said Herod. He lost the sweetness in his voice. "What did you see?"

"Sir, there were many of them. At least a dozen masters and another dozen servants, all of them on camels. Some of the beasts carried great packs, while the others just carried the masters and very little cargo."

"Good, good," said the King. "Here is a piece of silver for your troubles."

Then he casually asked another question.

"Was there an animal with a strange contraption on its back?"

He was careful not to arouse suspicion.

"Yes, sir," said the peasant, pleased by the gift of silver. "There was this funny thing on the back of one of the smaller camels."

As the poor man tried to describe the thing, Herod became impatient.

"Tell me, was there a small child in this thing?" he asked.

"A small child?" asked the peasant.

"Yes, a small child," said Herod. "A small child, very young, perhaps newborn."

Herod grew angry. He could no longer act polite and was having trouble controlling himself.

"No, sir," said the peasant. "There was no baby on that caravan."

"Are you absolutely certain?" asked Herod, more calmly.

"Yes. It passed close by me, as close as I am to you. I saw every one of them."

"No chance that you could be mistaken?" asked Herod, as he approached the now frightened man.

"No chance, your excellency," he said.

Satisfied, Herod looked him right in the eye.

"Tell no one you were here. And now, be off with you."

When the peasant left, the centurion stood at attention. Herod thought for a while. He needed to confirm what he had just heard, but he did not want to rely on only one report. He turned to the Gaius Cassius.

"Take some men and travel south toward Beersheba. I want confirmation that the Magi have gone that way. Send others along the military road to Samaria."

He thought for a moment about where else they may have gone.

"Send a few men to Jericho and some others to Caesarea Maritima. I want to know by the morning actually where they went. I also want men to be sent to the town of Bethlehem to learn the identity of the child the Magi were seeking."

He paused, then spoke sweetly.

"We too must pay particular tribute to this special one."

Herod turned and walked to the far end of the balcony. He was fuming. He looked out across the city and shouted to the stars.

"If I have to kill every boy under two years old, I will get this child. He will not live to reign in this kingdom or any other."

* * *

The Holy Family was tucked safely away in a small house in the southwestern corner of town. They told their relatives that they had to make a short trip. When asked where they were going, Mary told Joseph's cousin that an angel had appeared to Joseph. With that, the conversation ceased, and everyone looked at Joseph strangely; this was a family that was not inclined to believe stories about angels. Mary had deliberately chosen to share this so they would stop asking. Joseph and Mary wanted to sleep, but they politely stayed up to talk. Baby Jesus was already asleep. He never heard the conversation, and he never heard the storm.

This was not a night to be out in the Negev Desert. The wind started howling, and the clouds rolled in. No rain fell, but the air was filled with sand blowing from many miles away. Mary and Joseph wondered where the Magi were and if they were safe.

* * *

When the winds started, the Roman centurion wisely instructed his men to wait until morning before heading out in search of the Magi. He knew that wherever they were, they would not be traveling tonight.

Herod was drinking his favorite wine and thinking about the days of the great battles between the Roman legions and the Parthians. The Magi had to be aligned with the

Parthians. When the Emperor, Julius Caesar, decided to put an end to the uprising, he chose to install Herod as king. It was as simple as that. When Caesar decided something, it was as good as done. Now, in Augustus Caesar's reign, a Parthian king would not be tolerated, and he knew that. Would the Parthians try to take control of Judea and Samaria by installing a Jewish king? Rome would come down hard with an iron fist if the Parthians revolted. They would also come down hard on Herod for allowing it to happen.

Herod could not and would not tolerate that. The Parthians were traditionally educated by the Magi. He knew that there had to be some connection between the visit of the Magi and the political advantages sought by the followers of Antigonius, the Parthian. Herod had married Antigonius' daughter to bring about peace, but if the Parthians and Jews united under a Zoroastrian-educated Jewish king, he would be in trouble. He had already had some of the offspring of Antigonius' daughter secretly put to death to avoid future problems, but a Jew from the House of David would be far worse. He lifted his chalice to the stars and addressed the newborn King.

"May your death be a blessing to mankind. May it be as sweet as this wine."

* * *

The Magi continued eastward for many miles, eventually entering the land of Mohab. This barren land stretched to the east of the Dead Sea. It barely sustained sheep and had very few patches of farmland. The sparse vegetation consisted mainly of fruit and nut trees, but it was an easy land for the caravan to traverse.

Near the end of the day, Abdul and Nemir caught sight of the rest of the caravan. They hurried to reach the others. Neither relished the prospect of trying to get back to Persia without the others.

Gaspar was the first to speak to the two camel drivers.

"Were you able to get the two camels into the well?" he asked.

"Yes, sir," said Abdul. "I went into the basin myself, with both animals."

"And you were able to leave without them following you?" asked Gaspar.

"Yes. I tied the two beasts together so neither could climb out on their own."

"Actually," said Nemir, "The older camel looked as though she wanted to stay. It was like she knew that this was what she was supposed to do."

"Yes. It was the little one that seemed bent on getting out of the basin," said Abdul. "He was scared and tried desperately to climb out. After a while, he settled down."

Balthasar noticed the bolt of cloth and looked at Melchior and Gaspar with questioning eyes.

"Why was the cloth removed from the seat?" Balthasar asked.

"It was too large to allow the child to fit, so I put the Zoroastrian caps in its place," replied Abdul as he handed over the luxurious material.

"This belongs to the child," said Balthasar. "One day, it will have to be returned to its rightful owner. It was not yours to remove. The cloth may have had some purpose in his mission. You will have to return it."

Abdul looked at Nemir as if to say, "Once again, you got us in trouble."

"Yes sir, when you wish, we will return it."

* * *

The sun set more quickly in Makhtesh Ramon, in part because the steep walls blocked the last hour of sunlight. Tonight, there was something else. A storm was brewing and clouds brought darkness from the west.

Jamil knew the smell of a storm and this one smelled bad. It not only smelled bad but also had a strange feel to it.

The Negev Desert was a peculiar place. Because of the geography and the geological formations, a storm could indeed blow through and behave differently than anywhere else in the world. The basin was curved and if the winds came in from the right direction, the fury of the storm was amplified. If the winds reached a certain strength, they would pick up chalk powder and gypsum. When that happened, the air became drier, making it more difficult to breathe. Worst of all, everything became white, and it blinded you.

Jamil pulled on the tether to Heba.

"There is a storm brewing, and I don't feel safe in this Godforsaken place."

"Don't worry, Jamil," said Heba. "God will provide."

"He is going to provide us with a storm."

"That is true, but that is not necessarily a bad thing."

Heba tried to be supportive as she spoke with Jamil, but he wasn't accepting it.

"The Sustainer brings us adversity to stretch us a little."

"I've stretched enough, thank you," said Jamil.

"Yes, I am sure you have. Still, we must let the Sustainer decide what our adversities should be."

Heba searched for the right words to say but could say no more. She knew that Jamil wanted to complain. Heba rarely was at a loss for words, but she wanted something to ease the pain in her little friend's heart and felt unable to do so.

It grew darker much faster than usual. This frightened Jamil. He started to feel dizzy. Sometimes, when life was out of control and survival threatened, strange things happened. Resources that were hidden from view suddenly burst forth and enable one to survive, even flourish. Jamil was unaware of this. He simply felt threatened.

Like most camels newly acclimatized to the desert, Jamil had no idea what was in store for him. His only thought was that if he did not take control of the situation, something dreadful would happen. His problem was that he had no way of controlling it.

Heba knew the kind of turmoil Jamil was going to experience. She also knew that a powerful storm could transform Jamil and that if it did, there would be no returning to his original state. Once a camel's mind is stretched by the adversity of the desert, it never reverts to its original beliefs. Something inside snaps and the camel can never go back to the life of indulgence at the oasis. It needs the adversity of the harsh climate to feel complete. Its wholeness is manifested only when it is under duress. Jamil was going to learn about rising to his greatness. The desert was there to teach him.

"Life has the power to teach us things about ourselves that we had no idea existed," said Heba.

"Even when we're not sure we want to learn? Suppose I don't get it? It might be too complicated."

At least he was being honest about feeling inadequate for the task.

"The web of life is intricate. To fail to appreciate what a marvel life is, would be to throw away our gratitude and wonder."

"There you go again, Heba," said Jamil. "You're trying to teach life with philosophical descriptions. That drives me crazy."

Jamil was scared. The sky was growing dark, and the winds were blowing steadily now.

"Life will teach you what you need, even with me driving you crazy. You will end up filled with gratitude."

"I am tethered to a nut, a camel who wants to teach me about gratitude while I stand in a basin in a desert in the middle of nowhere. The wind is howling. There are particles in the air that irritate my eyes and nose. You want me to be more grateful?"

"Gratitude would help you see things a little differently," said Heba. "Sometimes a slight adjustment of viewpoint produces a fantastic new vision of things."

"A fantastic new vision of things? Well, I can't even see two feet in front of me with all this dust blowing. Every time I open my eyes wide enough, they get burned by the dust."

"Close your eyes, Jamil," said Heba. "Go inside and relax. As you relax, let go of your desire to see things with your eyes open."

"Now you want me to stand out in the desert with my eyes closed in the middle of a storm?" cried Jamil.

"Close your eyes," said Heba gently.

Jamil did so reluctantly.

"Don't do it to appease me," said Heba. "Do it to experience yourself more fully in this storm."

"I don't want to experience me more fully in this storm," said Jamil.

He opened his eyes just enough to peek at her.

"You don't have a choice, little one," said Heba.

He knew that he was stuck in the storm. He could play along. He was getting bored arguing with her.

"There is only one reasonable thing to do. You may try to avoid it with resentment, self-pity, and a few other tricks from your ego, but it must be done. Go into the experience. You need to lean into life and learn what it means to be you. Now close your eyes," gently commanded Heba.

As Jamil closed his eyes, Heba spoke in a soothing voice.

"Now let yourself relax into your belief in the Sustainer. Just be yourself in the storm. You will be okay. Let your faith hold you."

She waited for a moment until Jamil exclaimed in surprise.

"How is this possible? I can see! I can actually see!"

"Of course, you can see, Jamil," said Heba. "You are a camel, and you are blessed with the gift of sight in a storm. Yet while you protested your fate, you did not even know you could see with your eyes closed."

"But how is it possible?" asked Jamil.

"It is quite simple," said Heba. "You were given the gift of two eyelids. One set eliminates light so that you can

experience darkness when necessary. The other protects your eyes from flying sand and debris."

"Marvelous!" said Jamil. "It's as though the desert storm and I were two old friends. It's peaceful."

"Oh, but you are old friends," said the wise camel. "The desert's winds have blown for millions of years. For all that time, the camel has been blessed by the Sustainer so that he may survive, nay, even thrive in the desert."

"I feel so at home right now," said Jamil, "and serene. This feels like the most natural thing in the world. I'm standing here, in the midst of the wind's fury, with my eyes protected, and I can see almost as well as if my eyes were open."

"You have opened them even wider in another sense, little one," said Heba. "You have just experienced an important spiritual principle."

"What is that, Heba?" asked Jamil. His voice was peaceful. The fear was gone.

"When you first trust in the Divine, then all things will be given to you."

"That means?"

"It means that all your needs are taken care of by the Sustainer. Even before you know what to ask for, the Divine is preparing to deliver the desires of your heart. The infinite mind of the all-powerful Sustainer gives you everything you need for your life's tasks."

"But I didn't even know I had two pairs of eyelids, let alone realize that I might need them in a desert storm," said Jamil.

"That's right," said Heba.

"How could the Sustainer know my need before I knew to ask?"

"If you are willing to trust God in directing all your affairs, then you will discover what hidden gifts you have been given. The Sustainer has blessed every life form with astounding talents," said Heba.

"How do I discover these hidden talents?"

"The proper set of circumstances will unleash the hidden potential within you. All you need is the right challenge and the faith that it is meant to build you. Suddenly, you will discover something new about yourself."

"I want to learn more," said Jamil. "This is so peaceful. It feels so right, almost as though I was meant to stand in this storm with my head held high. I feel as though I belong. Yes, that's it... I belong."

"You have come home, little one," said Heba. "The desert and all its adversity are home to you. You need nothing more than to let yourself experience what comes to you with love and joy. Then you will find that you, too, have special gifts."

"Like what?" asked Jamil.

"Like the ability to hear the Sustainer's will for you in the whisper of your heart."

"You mean I'd be able to hear where the Sustainer wants me to walk in the desert?"

"Precisely. Once you understand the Sustainer's will, your life takes on ease and serenity."

"I'll know where the Sustainer wants me to go?"

The idea excited Jamil.

"How will I do that?"

"The how is simple, Jamil," said Heba. "How is by being honest, open-minded, and willing. It is as simple as surrendering to the Sustainer's will."

"That doesn't tell me how, Heba. That tells me what."

"Let me simplify it for you. First, look around at all the turmoil here in the desert. Our problems have increased. Our situation is as bad as it can be. Yet, you feel my enthusiasm for our future, can't you?" asked Heba.

"Yes, I can. You're more excited now that a storm has started."

"Exactly. I was excited when they left us down here in the basin. You were frightened. I was peaceful and serene. From the depths of my soul, I could hear the Sustainer whispering that I was to go down into the basin and wait."

"I wanted to leave. I was scared that it would be too difficult down here."

"You were afraid for your life, little one," said Heba, "And I was discovering mine. For you, it was chaos, and for me, it was divine order. Sweet, serene, ever-supportive divine order was enfolding me, and carrying me down into the basin."

"And for me, it was fear dragging me to my demise."

Jamil looked around again. He was so much more peaceful now with his eyes closed. He did not believe anything bad was going to happen.

"I feel as though I'm beginning a very joyful journey."

"And you are my friend. You are on a journey to find your purpose. It will be the most effortless journey you will ever take."

"Why will it be so easy?" asked Jamil.

"I didn't say it would be easy," said Heba, "just effortless. It is simple, not easy. It's effortless because it does not require your will. It requires you to follow the Sustainer's will."

"There is more work to be done, isn't there?" asked Jamil.

"There are always some tasks to be done, but when they are done with total surrender, it will not be work as you know it. It is more like love or joy or a dance with the Divine," said Heba.

The storm was now reaching its peak. Heba wanted him to get on with the lesson.

"No more questions," she said. "Be quiet and listen to the fury of the wind. Do you hear how loud it is?"

"Yes," replied Jamil.

"You won't find God in the howling fury," Heba said.

"No, it just makes me a little more afraid."

"See the lightning? Hear the booming thunder?"

"Sure."

"You won't find God listening there either," Heba said.

"What . . . where do I listen?"

"Listen to your thoughts. Notice how you can still hear them, no matter how loud the noise of the outside world gets."

"Yes, they are still there," said Jamil.

"Notice how your thoughts come as a stream with only the tiniest gaps between them. Sometimes they come so fast that you can't even notice the pause between thoughts."

"Okay, I see what you mean."

"Listen carefully to the silence between the thoughts. Still your mind and let the thoughts slow down."

Heba paused to give her young friend some time.

"What do you hear when you listen to the silence between your thoughts?"

"There is the sound of a hum, very soft and far away, coming from the core of my being," said Jamil.

"That's right. That is the sound of the life force within you," said Heba. "Now listen until you are certain you can follow the sound down to the depth of your soul."

"I don't know what that means, 'follow it to the depth,'" said Jamil.

"Be patient. This is what you need to do. Pick your favorite name for God. What is it?" asked Heba.

"Sustainer," said Jamil.

"Good. Now, say the name 'Sustainer I trust in you' deep inside your mind. Don't just say it, but release it into the space between your thoughts. Just let it go and follow it by gently observing where it goes when you release it."

Heba waited a long while. Normally, this would have been torture for Jamil, but he was so engrossed in watching where the sound went that he lost all track of time. What seemed like a few moments was much of the night. Deeper and deeper he went. Heba waited patiently in the stillness of her own heart, in union with the Divine.

A few times, Jamil was distracted.

"Return to the name you love so well," said Heba. "Gently and peacefully return to the thought that leads you back to the depths of your soul."

At one point, Jamil became frustrated with the stream of his thoughts and complained. "You should hear how crazy my thoughts are," he whispered.

Heba stopped him.

"Love everything you find inside you. Don't judge. Don't

criticize. When all is given to the Sustainer, all is used for your benefit, no matter what you think of it."

Jamil settled, even though he was aware of how terrifying the windstorm was. He was becoming even more peaceful. Something inside him was moving. It was as though an energy unlike any other he had ever experienced was building within him. He felt waves of joy that started in his back and ran up his spine. As each wave passed over him, he was filled with energy. His body was filled with bliss. He was tingling all over. It appeared as though it was happening to his body, and he was an outside observer. He was in another place and time, yet very much here, in the present. There was no past, no future, just the bliss-filled present. And then it happened.

From deep within him, Jamil heard, "None may keep the fulfillment of my promises from you."

He was softly startled. It was the sweetest voice he had ever heard, and yet it was the voice from his dream. The Sustainer was speaking to him from the depths of his soul. This time, instead of fear, he felt unbounded bliss.

"I can hear him," whispered Jamil. "It's as though he is right inside, way down deep in my being, speaking to me."

"He is, little one. His voice is the whisper in a camel's soul," Heba said.

"It is not exactly a voice. It is more like a knowing of his idea or ..." He paused, for he could not find the right word.

"It is a knowing of his will in the moment," said Heba.

Jamil knew that he knew. He knew it was possible to understand God's will for him, not in the abstract, but in a realistic and useful way. He also knew that the

understanding came from a place of peace and joy. It was a place of pure being, total awareness, and infinite bliss.

"It is an awareness that I am completely loved by the Sustainer."

"Once you understand that you are His beloved, then understanding the Sustainer's will for you is easy. All tasks are supported by his will and life becomes much simpler. You have the trust in the one who loves you completely as a little child has in the arms of his father."

Jamil was quiet. There was no need to talk, only to be. His serenity was as profound as the storm was furious.

"We must start to walk now, Jamil," said Heba. "We do not need to be in Makhtesh Ramon forever."

"Where shall we go, Heba?"

"Go inside and ask, and I shall follow, trusting that the Sustainer will provide an interesting journey for us."

"This way then, my friend," said Jamil.

"Remember to love every part of the journey as a gift from the Sustainer. When you love all things as the Sustainer does, then the next lesson begins."

"The next lesson is the miracle of unfolding purpose. You will see that your purpose in life is as easy to live as it is for a flower to bloom."

They walked off into the distance side by side, silent in the storm.

Matthew 2:16
"When Herod realized that he had been deceived by the Magi, he became furious. He ordered the massacre of all the boys in Bethlehem and its vicinity two years old and under, in accordance with the time he had ascertained from the Magi."

19

THE HOLY INNOCENTS

Herod awoke with a start. He dreamt that he cut his hand. The dream was unclear since the effects of the past night's wine left him less than clear-headed, but he was perturbed. As he rose from his bed, he ordered the slaves to draw his bath and sent for a priest. He wiped his hands on the bed sheet. He could feel the blood, but none was there.

The priest arrived presently. His court never keeps Herod waiting. When the priest entered, Herod pushed away the grapes he was being fed.

"I had a disturbing dream this night. I need some answers. I must decide what it means and act upon it at once!"

His emotions were getting out of control. Fear and anger were welling up inside him. The servant grabbed her grapes and backed away.

"I am at your disposal, sir," said the priest. "Please tell it to me."

There was the usual dread that accompanied a request from Herod to interpret a troubling dream.

"I'm having some difficulty remembering it all. But in the last scene, I picked up some tiny stars and crushed them in my hands. There was an incredible feeling of delight as I squeezed the blood from them. I tried to wash my hands and I couldn't get the blood off. I feel dirty."

"I see," said the priest.

Herod could tell that the priest didn't see at all. He was stalling, which aggravated him more than if he had just admitted that he didn't know.

"What do you think it means?" demanded Herod.

The priest continued to hesitate.

"Get out and get me someone who knows, you imbecile," shouted Herod. He threw a wine glass at the man.

The priest backed away and then hurried out the door. He ran down the corridor, calling for the other priests to go to Herod's chambers. It would be a couple of days, however, until Herod or the priests understood the full significance of the dream.

* * *

Joseph woke long before dawn. In his dream, he had been in a desert, looking for a small basket for Jesus. When he found it, he placed the baby inside and started walking toward Egypt. He realized it was the same papyrus basket that Moses' mother placed him in to float him on the Nile.

Joseph rubbed the sleep from his eyes and looked around the room he was in, half hoping that there would be a basket for Jesus. He decided that they must head into the desert today. Joseph was unsure of which route to take to Egypt. The road from Beersheba to Raphia was farther to the south than the road to Gaza. It would be a much more difficult trip, however, because the southern route passed through the Negev Desert. This was the same desert Moses had wandered through for forty years. The Roman territory of Herod did not extend that far south, and it would be safer. He knew that he must take the road to Raphia.

Mary stirred in bed next to him.

"Mary, we should leave before the sun is up and head south," whispered Joseph.

She immediately knew they were going to the desert.

* * *

Roman soldiers were leaving Jerusalem on horseback. They quickly would reach all parts of Herod's kingdom. In only a few short hours, Herod would have the information he so desired.

Herod was kept busy with more census information. He had to have his tax accountants regulate the collections to match the census reports he sent to Rome. This was important business, and he was careful to be as accurate as possible. He kept as much of the tax revenue as he could justify. Any inaccuracy could be his ruin. He was distracted from this important business each time a horseman arrived at the Hasmoneam courtyard.

A few hours later, the first report came back from Bethlehem. The centurion presented the information to Herod.

"The family of the child departed yesterday, probably heading south, as far as my men were able to tell," said the centurion.

"Are you absolutely certain that they were heading south?" asked Herod.

"No sir, we are not, but we have identified the family. I can verify that they have relatives in Nazareth, to the north," said the centurion. "The census officials were extremely helpful."

"Yes, of course," said Herod.

He pondered the centurion's report. If the Magi went

south, then he should have his men look for a family traveling with a camel holding a strange harness. If they went north, then he should have his men looking for a family with a small child.

"Let's await the reports from Beersheba and see if they did indeed, go south."

* * *

The sun had not yet risen in the Negev. Jamil was enjoying himself thoroughly, following the directions of a voice that had once terrified him in his dreams. He was wandering around Makhtesh Ramon, filled with joy, living totally in the now. He was traveling one step at a time with a slow and easy cadence. The experience was serene. He was peaceful, living as a camel must, roaming the desert with a strange load on his back. His turmoil was gone, and he was emptied of his fears. His obsession with water was gone. He was following a will far greater than his own. His life was in harmony with the will of the Sustainer.

"Don't you wonder where we are going?" asked Heba.

"Not exactly. Rather, I am marveling at the beauty of the voyage. I'm curious to find out where it will take me, but I need not know."

"Ah, you are feeling it?" asked Heba. "You have gotten into a flow with the Divine, and life is a peaceful journey of discovery."

"I know that living the journey well is important because the final destination is always back to the Sustainer."

After hours of wandering, they walked up a gradual incline that would lead them out of the basin. They both anticipated something wonderful. Without projecting into

the future, they enjoyed each step, even the obstacles they faced.

For Jamil, the desert and all of creation had become his friend. Every step of his path was a small gift from the Sustainer. His life had become an unfolding adventure of love between his nature and the elements of God's creation.

* * *

The Holy Family was moving slowly along the road that led to Raphia. It was hot and dry, even at this time of the year. This was a difficult trip, even under the best of circumstances. Joseph was worried about the toll it would take on his young wife and child.

Mary was grateful that her baby was doing well. He was peaceful and content. As she marveled at how beautiful Jesus was, Joseph interrupted her thoughts.

"Mary, I hope I have not made a mistake in coming this far south into the Negev."

"I have faith that if we are on the wrong path, God will intervene and direct us," said Mary.

"I suppose you are right, but it seems such a difficult path to follow, and . . . "

Joseph started to say something else and then stopped.

Mary sensed that there was something else.

"What is it you wish to tell me, Joseph?" she asked.

"Mary, I wish you had not refused the gift of the camel."

He was embarrassed to mention it, but he regretted her decision.

"Would it have been that much of an aid to us?" she asked.

"Only in this part of the journey. In the first part, it

would have been so peculiar that we would have stood out wherever we went."

He looked at her lovingly. There was no need to make her feel bad.

"It was only one camel and the journey would not have taken any less time because we could only travel as fast as the donkey."

She was distracted by the striking scenery of the Makhtesh Ramon basin. Joseph noticed her fascination with the various formations.

"Let me tell you the legend of this basin."

* * *

When the report came from Beersheba that the Magi had left two days before, Herod was furious. He needed to question the Magi about the exact location of the child. It incensed him that they had left and had taken another route. By now they were in the land of Mohab and obviously out of his grasp. But he did not spend much time worrying about where they were. He was almost certain that the child was not with them. He had to find the child.

The centurion reentered Herod's chambers.

"We have news, sir," he said.

"Yes? Quickly, out with it," said Herod.

"The Magi have left Beersheba with the special camel and the child seat. There was still no child in the caravan."

"Are you certain?" asked Herod.

"Absolutely," said the Roman soldier. "We have multiple reports that the Magi left without the child."

"Anything else?" demanded Herod.

"Yes, sir, we have a few reports that the family was poor and only owned an ass."

"Good. Then they will most likely be traveling slowly," said Herod. He looked out over the city and rubbed his hands. They suddenly felt dirty, and he absentmindedly rubbed them on his robe.

"Get me a scribe," he ordered. "I wish to issue a decree at once."

A scribe was brought in and Herod started to dictate.

"By order of King Herod, it is decreed that all first-born sons of Jewish parents in my kingdom below the age of two years will be immediately put to death."

He smiled, strangely pleased with the order. It was so reminiscent of the plague on the Pharaoh's lands. He felt like God almighty, creating his Passover. *I'm sending my own angel of death.*

Gaius Cassius grimaced at the thought. As a father, he hoped the decree would not be carried out, but he knew that the fate of many babies was sealed with this decree.

Herod paused for a moment and then addressed the soldier. "Make sure your men know to look for a family of three traveling with a donkey."

A few minutes later, soldiers were sent to all parts of the kingdom to complete this bloody task. It lasted for days and burned into the hearts and minds of the people. Herod would never be able to clean the blood from his hands, even though he would wash them repeatedly every day until his death.

Psalm 24:3
"Who can ascend the mountain of the LORD? or who may stand in his holy place?

20

THE LAST GIFT RECEIVED

The night sky was clear, as so often occurred after a tempest. It was cool and a good night for sleep. Gaius Cassius could not sleep, however. He was haunted by the thoughts of what his men were now doing. He had reasoned that a walk out to the Mount of Olives before sunrise would settle his mind and ease his heartfelt burden. He looked back across to Mount Sinai and Jerusalem. It was a beautiful city on a hill. One could barely see it, though, at this time of night. A few candles, the large Roman variety, burned near the palace, temple, and barracks. All else was shrouded in darkness.

The centurion gazed up at the sky. Heaven was majestically speckled with brilliantly blazing stars. There were millions of them in the Via Lactea or Milky Way. All were in their perfect place, moving as they were destined. He believed that the gods commanded the movements of the heavens and that the stars obeyed just as Caesar's legions obeyed his commands.

Gaius understood discipline and honor. He was a good soldier, loyal to Caesar, unafraid, and tested in battle. He had been trained to choose duty over dishonor. He reviewed his life in the military and the sacrifices he had made to serve in the Roman Legions. It was not constantly glorious, but it was invariably honorable. This was the first time that he felt he had followed a dishonorable

order. After tonight, he decided that he would transfer to another legion, perhaps Egypt.

His thoughts, however, wandered. They inevitably returned to his wife and children and to what kind of husband and father he was. It was difficult being away so often. He rationalized that he was protecting his children by serving Caesar. He was protecting all the children of the Roman Empire by preserving law and order.

He noticed that a few stars had flickered out. *How odd*, he thought. Then a few more faded and died. It was not yet daybreak. Was a thin cloud blocking his view?

Suddenly it hit him like a fist in his stomach. These little stars were dying. His heart broke. He watched with horror; his gaze frozen on the heavens. The tears of a shamed father burned his cheeks. He heard a sweet voice say, "Blessed are those who mourn, for they shall be comforted."

He did not feel blessed or comforted.

It had begun. Thousands of stars flickered out and died.

* * *

The sun blazed brilliantly as the two camels slowly made their way out of the basin. For the past few hours, Jamil had walked quietly, listening to the sweet silence within. He had become still while active. Life had changed, though nothing was different. The desert still glistened in the brilliant sunlight. It shimmered with the heat of the sun's rays, but now seemed even shinier. The expanded brightness made everything appear special. He was experiencing the reality of the Sustainer in everything he perceived. God was making His presence evident in all Creation.

Climbing the path upward to the top of the basin was not easy for the two camels tethered together. Yet, they were moving upward in a slow, precise, and steady manner. They had to slow down at times to negotiate the turns. The incline was so steep at some locations that the camels had to shorten their gait to keep from sliding backward. At this part of the journey, Jamil did not chatter or complain. He was patient for the first time in his life.

The presence of the Sustainer was everywhere. Finding this presence within himself had opened up his vision to see God in everything. It was as if he had developed a new vision of the Divine and all the world was within it. He had become one with this vision. His being had merged into a divine ocean of love. It was profoundly humbling.

When he looked at Heba, Jamil could see the divine presence in her. It was not that she had physically changed, but somehow his perceptions had. He could also see the hand of God in the desert flower and even in small insects. He wondered why it had taken him so long to get it. A part of him had always known the truth that he was now experiencing. Somehow, he had lost touch with who he was. This knowledge was an unaccustomed power for Jamil's soul. He was an infinitesimal drop in that ocean of love. His substance, his essence, was of the same stuff as the Sustainer. If fact, all of creation was made in and of the Sustainer. How could he ever have doubted this? How could he ever have thought the world did not support him? The desert was not his enemy. Learning not to drink was a blessing, even though it had been torture for so long.

He had discovered himself by living in the harsh

environment that he thought would drive him crazy. The key that allowed his true nature to unfold was letting go of what he thought he needed most. He had let go of his belief that the oasis was his salvation. He found that everything he needed to survive was given to him. He had released the desire to drink. More than that, he had given up the belief that water was the answer to life's problems. He actually could live without it. When he surrendered and let the Sustainer guide his will and life, he was filled with joy.

It was strange, though, because the feelings he experienced in the heat of the desert were more joyful than anything he had ever felt before. He knew that God was infinite goodness. He knew that it was part of the divine plan that certain animals were created to live in the desert, to be filled with joy, doing what others would not or could not do. Camels were created to live without certain pleasure so that they could experience the pleasure of the Sustainer in every act of their lives.

"Heba, may I ask a simple question?"

"Of course, my friend. You have been quiet for so long."

"The feeling..."

"The feeling has lasted, hasn't it?"

"Yes. In fact, it has intensified," said Jamil.

"I can hear the peace in your voice," said Heba.

"I am in awe. Everything in creation is part of His will, isn't it?"

He did not need an answer, because deep within himself, he knew it was true.

"I know that you know, little one," said Heba. "You never expected it to be so simple. Easy does it and the power of the Sustainer is yours."

"I feel so humble. I get what you mean by powerless, yet I am so filled with the presence that I have no fear."

"That is exactly how it is. You have discovered that God's infinite love is holding you in His hands. All power and glory are His, and yet the strength of the Sustainer moves your every step."

"There is awesome strength in surrender," said Jamil.

"Yes, there is," said Heba. "You could not feel it until you become more willing. You did not know what to do or how to do it. You just decided to experience whatever would happen by going inward. And there, you met the essence of your soul."

"I am certain that my life's purpose will be revealed to me as easily as walking up this slope," said Jamil.

"And you don't need to rush it. It will come in God's time."

"That's perfect timing too," said Jamil joyfully.

They continued to climb, slowly and deliberately, toward the top of the basin.

"I have one other question," said Jamil. "You told me that you would reveal what your name means. I had forgotten to ask, even though I wondered from time to time."

"It means gift from God."

"You are a gift from God to me, Heba. I can see that now."

"It's more than that, Jamil," said Heba. "No camel ever learns the lessons that you did all by himself. The Sustainer always sends a teacher, a gift from God."

"You have been patiently trying to teach me all along, haven't you?" said Jamil.

"Yes, but not just for your sake. The only way I can keep

the secrets of camel fulfillment is for me to give them away. You can never keep any of this if you do not pass it along."

"One day, I may help another camel develop their inner vision and to discover their true potential."

"That is exactly how it works. But first, you still have one more phase of the teaching to learn."

As Heba finished speaking, they both heard the braying of an ass in the distance.

* * *

Mary stood back, holding the child in her arms. The ass brayed in protest, refusing to go any further.

Joseph was frustrated. He did not know what to do. He did not want to stop and unload the ass, because he wasn't sure it would continue without the bundle it was carrying. He also did not want to leave anything in the desert, because it would mark their trail. They had come too far to start leaving tracks for the Roman soldiers to follow.

Then, as though it had a mind of its own, the ass started to walk again. Instead of walking on the road, it started directly south, toward the lip of the basin. Joseph was convinced that this poor little donkey, who had served the Holy Family so well, was finally going crazy. Maybe it was the heat or the strange terrain. Whatever the reason, Joseph did not care. He tried to pull the animal back toward the road. It was obstinate.

Mary walked a few steps behind at a safe distance. Under any other circumstance, this would have been funny, but she was concerned for the welfare of her husband and child. Then she saw the heads of the camels emerge over the edge of the basin.

"Joseph, look!" she cried.

Joseph turned just in time to see Heba and Jamil rise above the surface and walk up over the edge. He and Mary stood still as the camels continued to walk slowly toward them. Then, as they came within a few feet, the camels slowed and stopped.

Mary froze, not out of fear of the camels or for her son, but because the animals knelt, paying homage to her son.

Joseph looked at Mary.

Mary said, "Will wonders never cease? Look, they are now bowing down to our child."

"Yes, it does seem so," said Joseph.

"They were waiting for us."

"How is it that they knew where to leave the beasts for us?" he wondered.

"What should we do now?" she asked.

Joseph laughed.

"It's simple, woman. I will load our bundles onto the beasts. You care for the child while I do my work."

The task went quickly, for it was easier than he had expected to distribute the bundles on two animals. There was plenty of room. The animals were both strong, and the burdens were light for them.

As Joseph worked, Mary held Jesus and walked around the animals to watch. She started to talk to Jamil in a sweet voice.

"I hope you were not too upset that I didn't want you before, little camel."

She petted the shooting star blaze. Then she closely examined the child's chair on its side.

"I was frightened back in Bethlehem because you

seemed so big and dangerous to my child. I was not ready to accept you as a gift from the Magi, but I am now."

Joseph smiled at her. He tied down bundles on Heba's back, watching as she talked to Jamil. He whispered to Heba.

"It is not that she did not like your little friend. She just wasn't ready for this gift. She did not see how necessary he was for our child."

"It is too bad that the Magi aren't here, little camel," Mary said, "because I would say to them, on behalf of my baby, Jesus, I thank you for all the gifts you have given us. But I especially thank you for this little camel and the beautiful baby chair. I am sure my son will love it."

Joseph came over and took the child from her arms.

"Come, let me put him in the seat and see how he fits."

She reached in and pulled out the two Zoroastrian caps and gave them to Joseph. "I wonder why they left these."

As soon as the child was in the chair, she realized that it was a little too big for him. She tucked the caps along his sides to give a little extra support. The seat tilted back, and he laid still. It was perfect. Next, Joseph coaxed Mary up onto the part between the camel's humps. She was a little hesitant, but knew that she would have to do it. When she was seated on the soft, plush fabric, Joseph pulled on the reins. The camel slowly stood up.

Mary was delighted. It was thrilling to be up so high. She could see for miles. She had a wonderful view of the basin.

Joseph needed to get rid of the ass. It was an extra animal in difficult terrain. It would slow them down. He yelled at the ass and gave it a smart slap. It headed north. He

knew it would find its way to Beersheba. Joseph climbed aboard the older camel. It, too, stood up. Both had a little trouble adjusting to the swaying, but that was natural when riding on a camel. Jesus was gently rocked.

Joseph immediately pointed his camel toward the road. Heba and Jamil started at a pace that was much faster than the Holy Family had ever experienced. They would enter the Gaza strip in just a few hours. Raphia was only a short distance away by camel. They would be in Leontopolis long before midnight.

Mary called to Joseph as they rode.

"This is so fast. I can hardly believe how easy it is."

She looked at Baby Jesus, who was enjoying the swaying as the motion became regular. With each movement to and fro, he slipped gently into a sweet sleep. Mary's heart was filled with joy at the delight her child was feeling.

Joseph was relieved to realize that they would be safe. Egypt was just a short ride away. The desert would have no power over them now that they were on top of these two magnificent animals.

"The Almighty has provided us with a wonderful ride into Egypt, Mary," he said.

"And our Baby seems to enjoy it too," she laughed.

With each step, they drew closer to their destination, carried out of harm's way by the last gift of the Magi.

Matthew 16:25
*"For whoever wishes to save his life will lose it,
but whoever loses his life for my sake will find it".*

EPILOGUE

A CAMEL'S PURPOSE

They reached the Gaza strip in just a couple of hours. As soon as they were in Gaza, they were out of the territory ruled by Herod. There, he had no authority over the family. The angel had directed them to travel to Egypt. Joseph was just a few short hours from realizing the goal that the angel had given him. He was beginning to feel safe.

The road to Leontopolis on the Nile was an easy route to travel. Trade around the rim of the Mediterranean was active. Most travelers went unnoticed and these three, on two camels, were no exception.

* * *

"This part of the journey has been easy, hasn't it, Jamil?" asked Heba.

"Very. It is a good road."

"The end of the journey is drawing near, little one."

"I know, Heba," said Jamil.

He seemed like a different animal. Not that he had grown in stature, but somehow, he was changed. Both animals were aware of the transformation.

"It has been quite a time for you," Heba said.

"Yes, it has."

"You've learned many things, my friend," said Heba. "A journey is a strange thing, though. It begins by taking the

first step and ends with an understanding of the whole voyage."

"We draw closer to Leontopolis. Heba and I thought that by the time we arrived, I would know what my life's purpose is," said Jamil.

"You could know if you ask the Sustainer."

"It's that simple?"

"Yes, just ask," said Heba.

Jamil stilled his mind. He kept moving one step at a time. In the depths of his soul, he asked the Sustainer, "How can I know the true purpose of my life?"

He waited. A voice within spoke sweetly.

"Just look at who you carry, my child."

About Louis A. Tartaglia M.D.

In all his endeavors, Dr. Louis A. Tartaglia has devoted himself to helping others discover their purpose in life and uncover their hidden potential.

He is a Sleep medicine specialist, creative writer and inspirational speaker. He is the author of several books, including *Flawless*, the *Great Wing* and *Heart to Heart*. He lives in Sylvania, Ohio with his wife Jeanne and in his spare time coaches Fencing.

In the past he has practiced Psychiatry and Addiction medicine, and helped set up a rehab for Mother Teresa in Rome, Italy and Chihuahua, Mexico.

www.ingramcontent.com/pod-product-compliance
Lightning Source LLC
LaVergne TN
LVHW020926090426
835512LV00020B/3224